LIABILITY AND COMPENSATION FOR NUCLEAR DAMAGE

An International Overview

NUCLEAR ENERGY AGENCY
ORGANISATION FOR ECONOMIC CO-OPERATION AND DEVELOPMENT

ORGANISATION FOR ECONOMIC CO-OPERATION AND DEVELOPMENT

Pursuant to Article 1 of the Convention signed in Paris on 14th December 1960, and which came into force on 30th September 1961, the Organisation for Economic Co-operation and Development (OECD) shall promote policies designed:

- — to achieve the highest sustainable economic growth and employment and a rising standard of living in Member countries, while maintaining financial stability, and thus to contribute to the development of the world economy;
- — to contribute to sound economic expansion in Member as well as non-member countries in the process of economic development; and
- — to contribute to the expansion of world trade on a multilateral, non-discriminatory basis in accordance with international obligations.

The original Member countries of the OECD are Austria, Belgium,Canada, Denmark, France, Germany, Greece, Iceland, Ireland, Italy, Luxembourg, the Netherlands, Norway, Portugal, Spain, Sweden, Switzerland, Turkey, the United Kingdom and the United States. The following countries became Members subsequently through accession at the dates indicated hereafter: Japan (28th April 1964), Finland (28th January 1969), Australia (7th June 1971), New Zealand (29th May 1973) and Mexico (18th May 1994). The Commission of the European Communities takes part in the work of the OECD (Article 13 of the OECD Convention).

NUCLEAR ENERGY AGENCY

The OECD Nuclear Energy Agency (NEA) was established on 1st February 1958 under the name of the OEEC European Nuclear Energy Agency. It received its present designation on 20th April 1972, when Japan became its first non-European full Member. NEA membership today consists of all European Member countries of OECD as well as Australia, Canada, Japan, Republic of Korea, Mexico and the United States. The Commission of the European Communities takes part in the work of the Agency.

The primary objective of NEA is to promote co-operation among the governments of its participating countries in furthering the development of nuclear power as a safe, environmentally acceptable and economic energy source.

This is achieved by:

- *— encouraging harmonization of national regulatory policies and practices, with particular reference to the safety of nuclear installations, protection of man against ionising radiation and preservation of the environment, radioactive waste management, and nuclear third party liability and insurance;*
- *— assessing the contribution of nuclear power to the overall energy supply by keeping under review the technical and economic aspects of nuclear power growth and forecasting demand and supply for the different phases of the nuclear fuel cycle;*
- *— developing exchanges of scientific and technical information particularly through participation in common services;*
- *— setting up international research and development programmes and joint undertakings.*

In these and related tasks, NEA works in close collaboration with the International Atomic Energy Agency in Vienna, with which it has concluded a Co-operation Agreement, as well as with other international organisations in the nuclear field.

Publié en français sous le titre :
RESPONSABILITÉ ET RÉPARATION DES DOMMAGES NUCLÉAIRES
UNE PERSPECTIVE INTERNATIONALE

FOREWORD

From the beginning of the civil nuclear power industry, it has been realised that the use of nuclear energy involves risks. While the chances of an accident are low, the consequences may be severe and spread across national boundaries. This is why the countries of western Europe, when their nuclear industries were first being established, joined together to create an international regime governing liability and compensation in the case of a nuclear accident – the *1960 Paris Convention*, later complemented by the *1963 Brussels Supplementary Convention*. This initiative was soon followed by the adoption of the *1963 Vienna Convention,* which aimed at worldwide coverage.

More than 20 years later, the first nuclear accident with major transboundary consequences occurred at Chernobyl, and led to a fundamental reappraisal of the international liability and compensation regime. This reexamination is still under way.

The situation has been both an incentive and a complication for publishing this study. It has been an incentive because of the wide interest in nuclear liability, triggered by the Chernobyl accident and the consequent revision of the regime. In response to this interest, this book describes for the general reader the international nuclear liability and compensation regime, selected national legislative systems and insurance arrangements.

The fact that the revision is not yet complete, however, means that it has been necessary to describe a regime in a state of flux. Negotiations began in 1989 with a view to amending the *Vienna Convention*, and creating a new supplementary funding scheme to increase the amount of compensation available to victims. Although it is not possible to list all the proposals put forward, or to predict with absolute certainty which will eventually be adopted, the chapters on the subject aim at identifying the general trend of ideas and debate.

The Secretariat of the Nuclear Energy Agency is grateful to the European Insurance Committee for its co-operation in the preparation of this study.

The report is published under the responsibility of the Secretary-General of the OECD, and the views expressed do not necessarily correspond to those of OECD Member countries.

* * *

The Secretariat of the OECD Nuclear Energy Agency wishes to thank Ms. Louise de La Fayette, an international lawyer with the Canadian Department of Foreign Affairs, for her invaluable contribution to the preparation of this report.

TABLE OF CONTENTS

Chapter I

INTRODUCTION

Today, nuclear energy plays an important role in the economy of many countries. Indeed, some countries depend on nuclear power for well over half of their electricity requirements. However, the use of nuclear energy is challenged, with some countries avoiding it altogether, with others freezing its development or gradually phasing it out. In general, the resistance to nuclear energy is due to public opposition and this opposition largely stems from fears of catastrophic accidents. Quite naturally, after the accident at Chernobyl, those fears increased dramatically.

There is no question that, while it can be beneficial, the use of nuclear energy also involves certain risks. If an accident occurs, the damage to persons, property and the environment can be quite substantial. This was demonstrated by the accident at Chernobyl. Two of the most striking aspects of the accident were the geographical extent of the ensuing damage and the refusal of the former Soviet Union to compensate the victims outside its boundaries. Even in western Europe, where there was no personal injury, many people suffered economic loss resulting from impairment of the environment and contamination of foodstuffs.

Of course, the first line of defence against accidents is prevention. After Chernobyl States with nuclear installations and the competent international organisations reinforced their nuclear safety programmes, and moved to assist in the enhancement of nuclear safety in Central and Eastern Europe. The second line of defence is emergency response, and States and organisations also took rapid action to improve their capacity and performance in relation to emergency response as soon as an accident has occurred. Finally, if an accident does occur and damage cannot be prevented, then the persons responsible must be required to repair the damage and compensate the victims. This is the function of nuclear liability law.

The Originality of Nuclear Liability Law

One of the most remarkable features of the development of nuclear liability law is that it not only accompanied, but in fact, preceded the inception of a civilian nuclear industry. The second unusual feature is that the system of liability is special: it differs from the common law and it accommodates the unique features of nuclear activities and the conditions under which they operate. Third, specialised insurance cover was also present from the beginning, in many cases before the laws were even passed. And, finally, the liability regime was internationalised, again from the very inception of the nuclear industry.

Even now, thirty years after its creation, the nuclear liability regime is still one of the very few international civil liability regimes for potentially hazardous activities yet in force. Indeed, the only other one currently in operation is that embodied in the international conventions on oil pollution damage sponsored by the International Maritime Organisation. These were adopted several years after the nuclear liability conventions and after a catastrophic accident had demonstrated that they were necessary. In 1972 was adopted the *Convention on International Liability for Damage Caused by Space Objects*, which implicitly covers liability for damage caused by nuclear power sources in outer space. However, that convention involves State liability, not civil liability, as the State(s) responsible for the space objects must themselves compensate the victim. The difference between State and civil liability is explained in Chapter VI.

Thus, the nuclear liability conventions were the first dealing with land-based hazardous activities, and to a certain extent, they influenced the development of subsequent instruments. Since the adoption of the nuclear conventions, most subsequent treaties on liability have expressly excluded damage caused by nuclear materials. Some of these conventions are noted in Chapter IV.

The Necessity for a Special Regime

Establishment of a legal regime governing nuclear activities was absolutely essential to the development of the nuclear industry. After the original research and development work by governments into the applications of nuclear energy, many countries considered that nuclear power would provide the additional energy necessary to support the reconstruction of their economies after the war, and to promote rapid economic growth. While some of these created State-owned industries, others wished to encourage private enterprise in the nuclear field. However, potential investors were reluctant to act because of legal uncertainty and fears of crippling liability claims if an accident should occur.

For, nuclear energy was known to entail risks, but just how serious was uncertain. As a consequence, some governments moved to fill the legal gap by adopting national laws governing nuclear activities, of which both safety and liability were an inherent part. States wishing to foster a nuclear industry were concerned, at the same time, to protect the operators of nuclear power plants from ruinous liability claims and to provide adequate compensation for the victims of an accident. To this end, they devised a special liability regime whose special features are described in Chapters II and IV. To support the legal regime, a custom-tailored insurance regime was required and provided. The main aspects of nuclear liability insurance are described in Chapter III.

National Legislation and the International Conventions

The earliest national liability laws were adopted in the United States in 1957 and in Europe in 1959. A selection of these laws is outlined in Chapter VII. Simultaneously, in the context of the relevant international organisations, States were negotiating nuclear liability treaties to govern the problem at the international level. These treaties were required to permit victims to recover compensation for damage caused by a nuclear accident occurring in another country, or in the course of the international transport of nuclear materials.

In 1960, the *Paris Convention on Third Party Liability in the Field of Nuclear Energy* was adopted under the auspices of the OEEC, the predecessor of the Organisation for Economic Co-operation and Development (OECD). Three years later, the *Brussels Convention Supplementary to the Paris Convention* was adopted to provide additional funding beyond the liability limit of the operator. Also in 1963, the *Vienna Convention on Civil Liability for Nuclear Damage* was adopted under the auspices of the International Atomic Energy Agency (IAEA). There is no supplement to the *Vienna Convention*.

Naturally, the legislation of the States parties to these conventions has to conform to their provisions; yet, the legislation of many States that are not parties conforms to at least some of the main principles. These are the following. First, the operator of the nuclear installation causing the damage is absolutely and exclusively liable to compensate the victims for the personal injury and the property damage that they have suffered. Second, the operator is obliged to hold some kind of financial security (usually insurance) to cover his liability, in most cases, up to a certain liability limit (in some countries there is unlimited liability). In addition, claims must be made within a certain time limit.

Problems Appear

Fortunately, for twenty years after the creation of the nuclear liability regime, there were no major nuclear accidents to test the appropriateness and the sufficiency of the system. Then, in 1979, the accident in the reactor at Three Mile Island in the United States exposed certain gaps in the compensation coverage. Before it was known that there was no release of radioactive material outside the plant, the Governor ordered a precautionary evacuation. It was also recognised that if there had been a release of radioactive material off site, the property damage alone would have been substantial. Thus, it was questionned whether liability limits were adequate.

In addition, the United States is not a party to any of the liability conventions and has its own special liability regime. In accordance with American practice, the American insurance companies paid compensation for expenses related to the precautionary evacuation. States parties to the international conventions realised that under their terms, expenses related to precautionary evacuations and other preventive or protective measures were not expressly covered by these conventions.

Several years later, the disaster at Chernobyl revealed even greater gaps and inadequacies in the international liability conventions, as well as in the national legislation of certain countries. The accident at Chernobyl caused many billions of dollars worth of damage, not only in the Soviet Union, but also throughout the rest of Europe. Outside the immediate area surrounding the site of the accident, most of the costs incurred resulted from the preventive measures ordered by governments to protect their populations from the hazards of ionising radiation. None of these costs were compensated by the former Soviet Union, as it considered that it was not liable, because it was not a party to any of the conventions.

Thus, several insufficiencies had revealed themselves. First, the liability limits under the conventions were much too low. Second, certain countries with insufficient safety controls in their reactors were not party to any of the international conventions. At the time of Chernobyl, the *Paris Convention* had 14 parties and the *Vienna Convention,* 10. The countries of Central and Eastern Europe (with the exception of Yugoslavia) were not party to either convention. Third, not all the damage that might be caused was covered under the conventions. In addition, experts noted that there were other inadequacies not involved in Chernobyl that should also be remedied, such as the very brief time limits and the cumbersome procedures for making claims. These and other problems are discussed in Chapters VI and VII.

Solutions Proposed

As a consequence, within the context of the IAEA and the OECD Nuclear Energy Agency (NEA), States began to study the possibility of concluding a new convention or improving the old ones. As a temporary measure to link the *Paris* and *Vienna Conventions*, which hitherto had existed in complete isolation, in September 1988, the parties to both the conventions adopted the *Joint Protocol Relating to the Application of the Paris Convention* and the *Vienna Convention*. The effect of the *Joint Protocol* was to enable victims in States party to either convention to recover compensation from an accident for which an operator in a State party to the other convention was liable. Furthermore, it was hoped that the existence of the link, coupled with the improvement of the *Vienna Convention* would induce more countries to join the regime.

Next, the members of the IAEA embarked upon a negotiating process to amend the *Vienna Convention* to remedy its deficiencies. At the same time, work began on the development of a new convention to provide additional funding once the operator's liability limit under the *Vienna Convention* was exceeded. As explained in Chapters VIII and IX, negotiations on both conventions are continuing. However, differences of opinion and approach among the different countries involved indicate that full agreement lies some time in the future. After the negotiations in Vienna are completed, consideration will be given to the question whether the *Paris* and *Brussels Conventions* will also have to be improved or replaced.

Now that the revision process has perhaps reached its mid-point, the time is appropriate to examine the existing conventions, the unresolved problems, and the proposed solutions.

Nuclear Share of Electricity Generation (31 December 1993)

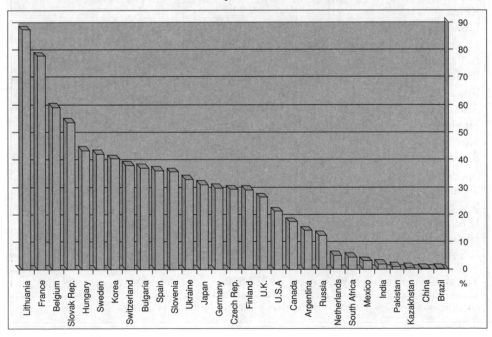

Source: IAEA.

13

STATUS OF NUCLEAR POWER AROUND THE WORLD
(31 December 1993)

Country	Reactors in operation		Reactors under construction	
	Number of units	Total MW(e)	Number of units	Total MW(e)
Argentina	2	935	1	692
Belgium	7	5 527	–	–
Brazil	1	626	1	1 245
Bulgaria	6	3 538	–	–
Canada	22	15 755	–	–
China	2	1 194	1	906
Cuba	–	–	2	816
Czech Rep.	4	1 648	2	1 824
Finland	4	2 310	–	–
France	57	59 033	4	5 815
Germany	21	22 657	–	–
Hungary	4	1 729	–	–
India	9	1 593	5	1 010
Iran	–	–	2	2 392
Japan	48	38 029	6	5 645
Kazakhstan	1	70	–	–
Korea	9	7 220	7	5 770
Lithuania	2	2 370	–	–
Mexico	1	654	1	654
Netherlands	2	504	–	–
Pakistan	1	125	1	300
Romania	–	–	5	3 155
Russian Fed.	29	19 843	4	3 375
South Africa	2	1 842	–	–
Slovak Rep.	4	1 632	4	1 552
Slovenia	1	632	–	–
Spain	9	7 105	–	–
Sweden	12	10 002	–	–
Switzerland	5	2 985	–	–
U.K.	35	11 909	1	1 188
Ukraine	15	12 679	6	5 700
U.S.A.	109	98 784	2	2 330
TOTAL	**430**	**337 820**	**55**	**44 369**

Note: The total includes 6 units, 4890 MW(e) in operation in Taiwan, China. Source: IAEA, 1994.

Chapter II

ORIGIN OF THE CONCEPT OF CIVIL NUCLEAR LIABILITY

The international liability regime relating to nuclear activities, as embodied in the relevant conventions, is a very special one, quite different in certain essential respects to the "common" or ordinary law that would be applicable in its absence. From the very inception of the nuclear industry in the late 1950s, States realised that a special regime would be necessary, both nationally and internationally, due to the hazardous nature of nuclear activities and the complexities of the processes involved.

Yet, while specifically tailored to the unique characteristics of nuclear activities, especially to the operation of nuclear power plants, nuclear liability law was not entirely novel. On the contrary, it was firmly based upon certain trends in national liability laws that had arisen in the late nineteenth century, and that in fact had their ultimate origins in Roman law.

This chapter will examine the conceptual basis of nuclear liability law in relation to the general principles of the law of responsibility for damage found in most legal systems, while Chapter IV will examine their precise realisation in the international conventions applicable in the nuclear field, and Chapter V will outline a selection of national laws on liability and compensation for nuclear damage.

Liability in General

Fault Liability or Strict Liability

The basic idea underlying liability law is that a person or entity responsible for causing harm to another should "make good" the harm or compensate the victim for the damage suffered. Ultimately, the idea is a moral one involving the concept of fairness or "equity", in that it is felt to be unjust that an innocent victim should bear the burden of a harm that was caused by another.

A simple example would be that of an accident in which a worker on a construction site violates a safety rule or makes a mistake that results in a heavy object falling onto a passing automobile, damaging the vehicle and injuring the owner. Because the worker was at fault, the construction company would have to compensate the driver for his injury and for the damage to the car. However, if the cause of the accident were not a worker, but a defect in a piece of equipment, such as a crane, then the manufacturer of the crane would be liable.

But how or why does the law determine that one person should pay for damage caused to another? There are two main theoretical bases for liability: fault or mere causation. In fault liability, the actor will be held responsible and will have to compensate the victim if he has breached a duty or has not conformed to a standard of care, either intentionally or through negligence. In the postulated example, this might mean that to save money, the construction company had deliberately ignored certain safety precautions, or that the individual worker had simply been careless or mistaken. From a moral point of view, one could say that it is only fair, just, or "equitable" that someone who injures another by his fault should pay for the consequences of his act. Otherwise, the innocent victim would have to bear the burden of the loss, which seems to be morally unacceptable.

In the case of the defective equipment, it is possible that there was a problem in the manufacturing process of which the manufacturer was not aware. That is, the manufacturer was not at fault, either negligently or intentionally: the defect was due to a phenomenon not under his control. Nevertheless, under the causal, "objective" or "strict" liability found in most legal systems in relation to manufactured products – the so-called "product liability" – the manufacturer would be liable, even if he were not at fault. Because the liability does not depend upon the behaviour of the actor, it is termed strict or objective. All that is required for the victim to obtain compensation is proof of causality, a causal link between his injury and the action of the defendant.

Even under strict liability, the actor may be able to avoid liability if there are certain extenuating circumstances which may "exonerate" him. Among the possible exonerations are *force majeure,* such as war or other hostilities, or an overwhelming natural disaster; the act of a third party either negligent or intentional; action by a public authority; the fault of the victim, etc. Generally, the extent of the exonerations is in inverse proportion to the degree of risk. If there are very few or no exonerations, then the liability may be termed "absolute".

Now, why should the actor bear the burden of the damage when he is not at fault? The answer lies in the special factual nexus of certain situations, in the economic relationships involved, and again in the fundamental notion of fairness or equity.

16

Historical Development

In the earliest stages of most societies, liability for damage was strict or objective, proof of fault was not required. If one person caused damage to another, then the actor was held responsible. Furthermore, that responsibility was collective. Before the development of a State structure with an organised legal system, justice was a kind of vengeance exercised between and by the private persons involved and their families. Eventually, a new approach developed based upon the perception of a person as an individual moral actor who must be held to account for his misbehaviour.

Under Roman law, individual responsibility was recognised, but the law did not usually require fault for a finding of liability and did not distinguish between civil and criminal law. A very early ancestor of the modern law of strict liability may be found in the Roman law regarding animals kept under a person's guard that caused damage to the person or property of another. The owner of an animal that caused damage was held to be strictly liable, and had to either compensate the victim for his loss or surrender the animal. The analogy lies in the fact that the actions of an animal are ultimately uncontrollable and that it may cause damage even if the owner himself is not at fault.

As time passed, in some countries rules developed to impose strict liability, or at least a reversal of the burden of proof in relation to damage caused by inanimate objects under someone's guard, and for things creating a special danger. The turning point in the development of strict liability came with the advent of the industrial revolution in the late eighteenth and early nineteenth century. For the first time in human history, machines and industrial processes began to be used that were virtually uncontrollable and that presented an ubiquitous danger to an extent previously unknown. There was both a greater risk that damage might be caused and a risk of greater damage.

Furthermore, due to the complexity of the equipment and its operation, the machines might break down or suffer an accident despite the taking of utmost care by the owner or operator and their adherence to all the relevant safety standards. In addition, the danger was depersonalised. In this new situation, there was no longer a single individual acting autonomously who might be held morally responsible for an act or a failure to act in accordance with the requirement of reasonable care, but a company operating through its employees and using machines. Because the company had overall control of an operation, including its safety aspects and in order that the victim might obtain compensation, the company had to be held responsible for an accident caused by an employee.

Finally, because the damage caused by an industrial process could be far greater than that caused by an individual human being, the amount of compensation required might exceed the ability of an individual or even a company to pay. As a consequence, entrepreneurs and companies began to rely on third party liability insurance to respond to possible claims for compensation.

Thus, there was a situation in which there was an unprecedented risk of great damage without any one person being at fault or being either factually or morally responsible. Furthermore, due to the technical complexity of the equipment and the processes involved and the industrial secrecy concerning their operation, it would have been difficult, if not impossible, for a victim to obtain the evidence necessary to prove negligence, even if the operator had indeed been at fault.

This new factual situation required a new legal response. A means had to be found to compensate third parties, innocent victims who had no connection to the source of the danger. Consequently, most legal systems devised a form of strict or objective liability, or at least a presumption of fault. Among the best known is the decision of the British House of Lords in the case *Rylands v. Fletcher* of 1868, subsequently followed in Commonwealth jurisdictions, as well as in certain of the United States.

In the original Exchequer judgement, Justice Blackburn declared:

> We think that the true rule of law is that the person who for his own purposes brings on his land and collects and keeps there anything likely to do mischief if it escapes, must keep it at his peril, and if he does not do so is prima facie responsible for all the damage which is the natural consequence of its escape.

On appeal, the House of Lords limited the basis of the decision to a "non-natural use of land" and to a harmful matter that had been kept under control and had escaped.

In France, the *1804 Civil Code* provides in Article 1384:

> One is liable not only for damage that one causes himself, but also for damage that is caused by persons under his responsibility or by things under his custody. [*Translation.*]

In actions instituted under this article, at first, the victim was required to prove the fault of the person keeping the thing under his guard, but in time the courts created a presumption of fault, quite similar to strict liability. All that is required is that the victim prove a causal link between the object and the damage. Laws of many other countries derived from the French civil code will contain similar provisions.

In other European laws, such as those of Germany, Switzerland and Austria, strict liability was provided for in separate laws governing particularly dangerous things. More recently, some countries, such as Germany, have legislated strict liability for environmental harm. In Japan, at the beginning of the 1970s, decisions in four environmental liability cases merged the concepts of fault and strict liability by applying the negligence provisions of the Japanese Civil Code, but placing a heavy burden upon the defendant companies to show why they should be excused from liability for the consequences of their activities.

A study prepared by the United Nations in 1984 demonstrated that similar concepts existed in most legal systems in Africa, Asia and Latin America, as well as all parts of Europe.

The Theory of Liability for Risk and the Concept of Equity

Strict liability is based upon the theory of liability for risk. Underlying the concept of risk, are the two notions of the possibility of something going wrong and the severity of the possible consequences. In a risky or hazardous activity, there will be an enhanced possibility either that an accident might occur or that the damage caused will be severe, or even both. In any event, the concept of liability for risk means that the person who created the risk is responsible and *will be held to account* for any injurious consequences. In fact, in the view of some commentators, the creation of a risk itself may be viewed as a kind of fault or "original sin".

In the case of an extremely risky activity, the government has two choices: either to ban it, or to allow it to be carried on only on condition that certain safety precautions are taken and that the operator assumes full responsibility for any injurious consequences. If, following a cost-benefit analysis, the government considers the activity to be economically and socially beneficial, it will permit the activity, subject to the requisite conditions, including that of the strict liability of the operator. This means the operator will be liable to compensate the damage caused to any victims without proof of fault.

The justification for imposing strict liability for hazardous activities is threefold:

- it is only fair or *equitable* that the person who creates a risk should bear the responsibility for any ensuing damage;

19

- the operator is in a position to control the risk and to take measures to prevent any accident; and

- the operator is in a position to get insurance to cover any compensation for damage.

Above all, it is considered to be *inequitable* or unfair that the innocent victim who has nothing to do with the activity or enterprise should bear the burden of the damage it causes. The person who creates and maintains the problem should be responsible for any untoward effects. In addition to these considerations of equity in placing the burden on the operator, there are economic reasons as well.

Economic Analysis

The economic justification for the strict liability of the operator is that he who benefits from the activity financially must accept the consequences and be responsible for any ensuing damage. That is, the entrepreneur who makes the profits must also take the losses and indemnify the victims for their injuries. In economic terms, the damage caused by an enterprise is one of its *costs*. In order for an economic activity to be efficient and to make proper use of the available resources, it should *internalise* its costs, that is, pay for all the costs itself.

If the activity causes damage to third parties and the victims have to bear the cost of the injury, then the operator of the enterprise is *externalising* its costs. In effect, he is allowed to cause damage for free and has forced a portion of his operating expenses on the victims. In a sense, the victims could be considered as subsidising the activity. In the light of the fact that the operator is gaining the benefit of the profits, this would not only cause economic distortion, it would also be inequitable.

The "Polluter-Pays" Principle

One might also consider the imposition of strict liability for damage caused by industrial activities as an extension of the "polluter-pays" principle (PPP). The concept was developed at the OECD in the context of the economic aspects of environmental protection to provide for the internalisation of the costs of preventing damage to the environment by an industrial activity. Originally, the principle referred only to the obligation of the "polluter", the owner or operator of the polluting activity, to internalise the costs of the damage by paying for pollution prevention measures required by the government. More recently, the principle was extended to accident situations by requiring the polluter to pay for the costs of emergency response and the mitigation of damage.

However, in popular usage, as well as in the context of other organisations, the principle has come to mean requiring the operator of the activity to pay compensation to the victims of pollution damage. The principle has been given legal substance by being referred to in a number of recent conventions, as well as being embodied in the new environmental provisions of the constitution of the European Community, the Treaty of Rome.

Safety and Prevention

There are three main purposes of liability law:
- compensation,
- the peaceful resolution of disputes, and
- deterrence or prevention.

Compensation has already been discussed and peaceful resolution has been hinted at. One of the social functions of the law is to provide a controlled means for the resolution of disputes so that injured parties do not take matters into their own hands. Historically, after the development of third party dispute settlement by a ruler or the courts, private vengeance was no longer necessary.

Deterrence or the prevention of accidents and therefore damage is the third, and not the least important function of liability law. If the operator does not have to pay the costs of the damage caused by his activity, then he will have little reason to exercise the safety controls necessary to prevent an accident. This is especially true if the safety measures themselves are expensive. Conversely, if he is liable for damage caused to third parties, the operator would have an incentive to take the utmost possible care.

The incentive would exist even if the operator were insured, as there are always costs that are not covered by insurance. Besides, the insurance company would not be willing to provide cover if it believed that the installation were unsafe, and premiums would rise should an accident actually occur. Thus, third party liability serves as a deterrent to carelessness and an incentive to safety.

Application to the Nuclear Field

Origins

In the mid-1950s, the governments of many industrialised countries viewed the development of nuclear power as a possibly limitless source of indigenously-produced energy that would enable their economies to develop rapidly and then usher in a new era of prosperity. However, fears of financially devastating liability claims in the event of an accident were inhibiting investments by potential nuclear operators and were causing suppliers and construction companies to refuse to accept contracts. For, under the ordinary law, both operators and suppliers would be subject to unlimited liability in the case of an accident.

The report "Theoretical Possibilities and Consequences of Major Accidents in Large Nuclear Power Plants" published by the U.S. Atomic Energy Commission in March 1957 estimated that damage to property from an accident could reach up to 7 billion dollars. Furthermore, the report concluded: "An inherently stable reactor is not completely immune to destructive runaways." In these circumstances, the reluctance of industrialists was understandable. The investment required would be considerable, and the losses even greater.

Above all, governments were concerned to protect operators from massive liability claims that could destroy their enterprise and put them into bankruptcy. Yet, at the same time, governments were also conscious of their responsibility towards the welfare of their citizens and of the need to ensure that they would be properly protected in the case of an accident. In the case of a catastrophe, thousands of people could be injured and their property contaminated. Some means had to be found to compensate the victims, without destroying the enterprise.

These conflicting interests, the benefits to the economy that might accrue from the development of nuclear power, the avoidance of ruinous claims for damages, and the need to protect the population, all had to be reconciled. Governments sought a solution that would encourage the development of the nuclear industry by removing the legal and financial impediments at the same time as providing adequate compensation for any damage.

In some countries, the solution was a government owned and operated nuclear power industry; in most, it was special legislation concerning nuclear activities in general and nuclear liability in particular. Due to a common perception of the risk and the requirements necessary to protect both the industry and the victims, the concepts underlying the earliest national legislation and the international conventions are quite similar.

Strict Liability

From the beginning, there was no doubt that the nuclear industry was a perfect example of the sort of activity in which the concept of *strict liability* for risk should be applied. Governments, jurists, operators and insurance companies, all agreed. Due to the unusual hazards posed by nuclear activities, it was acknowledged that permission to operate nuclear installations could not be granted unless the operator agreed to accept full responsibility for any injurious consequences. For, despite the utmost precautions, an accident could always occur and it was only just that the cost should be borne by the person who created the risk and not by the innocent victim.

Therefore, in all nuclear liability legislation (except that of the United States; see Chapter VII), the basis of liability is not fault, but strict liability for risk. Strict liability relieves the victim of the burden of proving fault or negligence, requiring the payment of compensation on mere proof of a causal link between the damage and the nuclear accident in issue. Since it would be virtually impossible for any victim to have detailed knowledge of what had taken place in the nuclear installation or in the course of the carriage when the accident occurred, strict liability is necessary for justice.

Furthermore, the exonerations would be limited to cases of damage caused directly by war or other hostilities, by an irresistible and unforseeable natural disaster, or by the fault of the claimant. In the law of some countries, the operator is not exonerated for damage due to natural disasters, because it was considered that the possibility of a natural disaster was within the risk and should be protected against by the operator. Similarly, the operator is not exonerated for damage caused by third parties, as he should foresee this possibility, including sabotage, and should take precautions against it.

For the same reasons, the operator should remain liable if a victim contributed to the accident through negligence. On the other hand, it would be unfair to make him pay compensation to a victim who had caused the accident intentionally.

Channelling and the Exclusive Liability of the Operator

At the initial stages of the development of the nuclear industry, suppliers and construction companies were afraid that excessive liability claims would ruin their business. For, under the common law, the suppliers or construction companies would be liable if an accident resulted from their fault or negligence. As a consequence, to encourage such companies to become operative in the nuclear field, governments introduced into their legislation the concept of "channelling" all liability to the operator. That is, the operator would be liable regardless of whose acts or omissions were the actual cause of the accident.

In addition to sparing suppliers and contractors the trouble and expense of defending a complicated and expensive liability suit, another reason for channelling all liability to the operator was the cost of insurance. For, if anyone involved in the construction of a nuclear power plant or in supplying components could be held liable, then all those parties would have to purchase very expensive third party liability insurance, even if nuclear activities constituted only a very small proportion of their business. It is possible that the insurance might even cost more than the business is worth.

For the victim, as a corollary benefit, the exclusive liability of the operator obviates the need to identify and to pursue the person who actually caused the accident. Due to the difficulty of obtaining the necessary evidence, this would be virtually impossible. Thus, with channelling, the victim would be able to avoid possibly fruitless and certainly expensive investigations and cross-actions.

In relation to the carriage of nuclear substances, there is also a derogation from the general rules on liability. Under the common law, a carrier is liable for damage caused during the course of carriage. However, this rule was considered inappropriate to the nuclear field as the carrier would also have to purchase expensive nuclear liability insurance, and because, in any event, he would not have been responsible for the packaging of the nuclear material and would lack the specialised knowledge of how to handle it. Therefore, in relation to the carriage of radioactive substances, it was considered both unfair and economically unfeasible to retain the liability of the carrier. Instead, liability would lie with the operator sending the substances, until responsibility were transferred to the operator receiving them or until the latter took charge of the shipment.

Compulsory Financial Security

In order to ensure that funds would actually be available to pay the claims, the provision of some kind of financial security was made compulsory. Usually, this security would be furnished in the form of third party liability insurance, but it could also be a bank guarantee or a form of self-insurance. In some countries a guarantee or indemnity is provided by the State.

The desire to protect the nuclear industry and the necessity of relying on insurance required both monetary and temporal limits on compensation. Although capacity for nuclear insurance has expanded greatly since the earliest times when insurers were uncertain of the risk, it still remains limited. Governments have generally been careful to stipulate a financial guarantee that does not exceed the capacity of the insurance industry, and for which the premiums would not be beyond the means of the operators to pay.

Limits on Liability

In the general law on liability there is no limit on the amount of compensation payable for damage caused by an accident: the person liable will have to pay the full amount, albeit within certain parameters related to the proximity of the causation. However, in the nuclear field, for the reasons outlined above – the desire to encourage the nuclear industry and to relieve operators of the burden of ruinous liability claims – most laws on nuclear liability provide for a limit on liability, which means a limit on the compensation payable in the case of an accident.

The limit usually coincides with the amount of financial security required, if not the insurance cover available. In other words, after a nuclear accident, even if the claims for compensation exceed the liability limit, the operator will only be required to provide funding up to that limit. Without a limit on liability, the operator would have to pay the balance from his assets. Yet, unlimited liability does not mean unlimited compensation, as no one has unlimited assets. If his assets all had to be disposed of in order to meet the claims, the operator would eventually be forced into bankruptcy, and out of business. Still, the victims might not receive much more than what was available under the insurance, as a serious accident might destroy the installation that was the operator's major asset.

Despite the practical impossibility of unlimited compensation, some countries have retained in their legislation the unlimited liability of the common law, as they do not see why the operators of nuclear installations should receive any special treatment. Because it is recognised that in the case of a major accident, the operator's insurance and even his assets may not be sufficient to cover all the claims, in most countries, the State will provide compensation beyond the operator's liability limit. If liability is unlimited, the contribution of the State will be made after the exhaustion of the insurance funds or the operator's assets.

Time Limits

For reasons of certainty, insurance companies have also limited their coverage in time, to not more than ten years from the date of the accident. Neither the insurance companies nor the operators could tolerate the prospect of remaining liable to pay compensation for an extended period of time, never knowing when a claim might suddenly arise. Hence, in some national legislation and in the existing conventions, the time limit for submission of claims is the same ten years. In addition, in most laws, there is a "discovery rule" requiring that claims be filed within two or three years of the discovery of the damage and the identity of the operator.

The Role of the State

Even before an accident occurs, the State has an important role to play in setting the conditions of the holding of financial security by the operator and in ensuring that the security is maintained. In some States, the security is a State guarantee or is backed by a State guarantee, meaning that if the security fails (for example, through the bankruptcy of the insurance company), the State will provide the funds required. In addition, this is required under some of the international conventions.

Given the various limitations on the liability of the operator outlined above, the question arose of how to fully compensate the victims in case the operator's liability were ineffective or insufficient. In the view of most commentators, and governments, the obvious answer was that the installation State should intervene. There were four basic reasons for this. First, the State was responsible for deciding to permit nuclear activities to be carried out in the first place. Furthermore, the State was responsible for supervising nuclear activities and for ensuring that they were conducted in the safest possible manner.

Third, the State was generally responsible for the welfare of its citizens, and for this reason customarily provided assistance to them in the event of natural disasters, such as floods or earthquakes. Hence, it was only natural to suppose that the State would intervene in the case of a nuclear accident, to succour the victims and to compensate them for the injury and damage suffered beyond the limits of the operator's liability.

Fourth, compensation by the State would amount to a social spreading of the risk in the interests of national solidarity. For, although the operator benefits from his activity financially through taking profits, the general population would also benefit from the electricity produced by a nuclear power plant or from the knowledge acquired through the use of a research reactor. If the State directly compensated the victims, the entire population would do so indirectly through the payment of their taxes. Since the entire population would have benefitted from the activity, it would be unfair for only a proportion of them to bear the costs of the inevitable damage.

Hence, in most national legislation, the State is required to compensate the victims if the claims exceed the limit of the operator's liability. Furthermore, in many national laws, the State will pay for the damage if the operator is exonerated, and in some, it will pay compensation for claims arising beyond the limitation period. As noted above, such intervention is only to be expected, due to the State's responsibility for the welfare of its citizens and the principle of national solidarity.

26

Finally, in certain States, the government will itself organise or control the process of compensation, in particular, if the cost of the damage exceeds the operator's liability limit. Further details on State intervention are provided in Chapter V.

Scope of the Special Liability Régime

The special liability regime for nuclear activities outlined above applies only to "nuclear installations" in which highly dangerous processes are carried on, such as reactors used in nuclear power plants, research reactors, factories for the manufacturing or processing of nuclear substances, factories for the separation of isotopes of nuclear fuel, and factories for the reprocessing of irradiated nuclear fuel. These processes are complex and hazardous in themselves, as well as involving nuclear materials which may react in such a way as to cause a major catastrophe. Also covered under national legislation and the international conventions are the transport and the storage of nuclear substances and waste. As for the final disposal of radioactive waste, most national legislation does not specifically mention it, nor do the international conventions. However, it has been decided that the *Paris Convention* covers the "operational phase" of final disposal. The issue of liability for damage caused by the disposal of radioactive waste is discussed in Chapter VII.

In the case of other uses of nuclear materials, such as radioisotopes used in medicine and industry, the risk is much lower and can be easily accommodated within the regular civil liability system. Similarly, uranium mining and milling is not covered by the special regime, as there is no danger of "criticality" or a sudden accident and the level of radioactivity is fairly low.

Chapter III

NUCLEAR LIABILITY INSURANCE

It would not be an exaggeration to say that the international regime of liability for nuclear damage would not exist in its current form if it did not rest on a firm foundation of nuclear liability insurance. Indeed, insurance was crucial in the development of the nuclear industry. Entrepreneurs would not have taken the risks they did had some form of financial security not been available to cover both material damage to their installations and compensation due through third party liability. In countries where governments have decided not to operate installations themselves and not to provide primary financial cover, nuclear insurance has been absolutely essential to ensure the development and the maintenance of the nuclear industry.

Furthermore, considerations of insurance were largely responsible for some of the specific aspects of nuclear liability law, such as the limitation of liability in amount and in time, and the channelling of liability to the operator. The amount of liability was limited because insurance capacity was limited. The operator's insurable liability was limited to ten years because of the difficulties foreseen in determining causation for cancers appearing perhaps twenty or thirty years after a nuclear accident; furthermore, the insurance industry would have been unable to provide compensation for such contingencies and it was considered inequitable to hold a nuclear operator potentially liable for such largely unprovable allegations. The operator had to be exclusively liable, so that the limited capacity of the insurance industry could be concentrated in one single policy instead of being dissipated amongst contractors or suppliers who would otherwise have required individual insurance protection from possible liability. For the same reason, rights of recourse were also limited.

One interesting aspect of the history of nuclear liability and insurance is that the earliest arrangements to provide nuclear insurance were made in 1956-57, just before the earliest national liability laws and a few years before the adoption of the international conventions. In fact, governments and the insurance industry worked closely together in the development of the liability regime, on both the national and international level. Throughout the years, this collaboration has continued with representatives of the insurance industry being consulted on changes in the law, especially with respect to limits on liability.

Moreover, the insurance industry cooperates on a continuing basis with States on the intergovernmental level, regularly attending meetings at the International Atomic Energy Agency and the Nuclear Energy Agency. In recent years, the industry has participated in the revision of the existing conventions, as well as in the negotiation of a possible new one on supplementary funding. These developments are discussed in Chapters VIII, IX and X.

Historical Background

In the late 1940s and the early 1950s, only governments were involved in the development of nuclear energy, for military purposes and in research facilities. Soon, however, governments realised the possibility of creating a nuclear power industry to provide an efficient and independent source of energy to fuel economic growth. While some governments decided to institute State-owned nuclear power programmes, others decided to leave the task to private industry, but with government encouragement. As noted in Chapter II, it quickly became apparent that investors were not going to venture into a virtually unknown and potentially dangerous field without the legal protection of a special liability law.

At the same time, insurance companies were also becoming aware of the importance of nuclear energy, but from the perspective of the potential damage resulting from an accident and the position to be taken by the insurance industry. Initially, the question was whether or not nuclear damage should be excluded from existing insurance policies, such as those for personal accidents, fire and explosions. From 1957 onwards – following the commissioning of the first nuclear power stations for the supply of electricity to national grids – insurers in various countries began to exclude nuclear damage from their regular coverage. If readers check their own insurance policies, they are certain to find a standard nuclear damage exclusion clause.

By 1954-55, there were thus three problems with one solution. It was clear that the nuclear industry would not develop without a special liability law. However, it was unlikely that compensation for nuclear damage to third parties could be paid by the operators out of their own resources, most of which would be invested in the installation. Secondly, if nuclear damage were to be excluded from existing insurance policies, how would the victims of nuclear accidents be compensated for their injuries and damage? There was also a related third problem. Who would pay for the devastating loss to the operator when an installation in which he had invested vast sums of money was damaged or destroyed in an accident?

The answer was obvious. The insurance companies would have to provide special insurance for the nuclear industry, both for material damage and for third party liability. The insurance policy would then serve as financial security from which the operator could compensate the victims of accidents occurring in their installations or during the transport of nuclear material. However, just as the unique features of the nuclear industry necessitated a special liability regime, so did they necessitate special arrangements for insurance. Around 1955-56, insurance companies in Europe and the United States studied the peculiar characteristics of the nuclear risk, coming up with arrangements that were broadly similar and remarkably prescient.

Problems Involved in Third Party Liability Insurance for Nuclear Installations

Providing third party liability insurance for nuclear installations was and, to a certain extent, still is a risky proposition for the following reasons:

- at the beginning, very little was known about the potential hazards of nuclear energy because it was an entirely new field;

- although the consequences of an accident could not be quantified, it was suspected that the total amount of damage might be quite considerable;

- the frequency of accidents was unknown and could not be predicted;

- little was known about the type of damage that might be caused;

- however, it was known that personal injury might only become manifest after the passage of a number of years;

- in most countries, there were only a small number of installations, thus limiting the number of potential policy-holders and the amount of premium income available on a national basis;

- the number of installations was relatively small worldwide, thus restricting the total amount of premium income available internationally;

- nuclear installations differed considerably in size, design and technology; and

31

–   the value of the installations and hence the material damage cover required was extremely high.

On the latter two points, it should be kept in mind that there are 32 States or other political entities with nuclear power programmes, and that of the 420 nuclear power reactors in operation in the world, just over half are insured. As the rest are operated by governments or government agencies, they are not required to provide financial security. In the late 1950s, no one could predict the future size of the industry and hence the number of potential policy holders.

In addition, due to the fortunately small number of nuclear accidents that have occurred, there is still not sufficient statistical data available to properly assess the risk on an actuarial basis. Furthermore, several years after Chernobyl, the long-term consequences of exposure to radioactivity on human beings and the environment are still not completely known, especially at lower levels of radiation dose.

Given the uncertainty about the nature and the extent of the risk, it is hardly surprising that insurers hesitated somewhat before deciding to plunge into the nuclear field. Yet, they did not hesitate for long, in part because there was some pressure from governments and the nuclear industry to provide the necessary cover. When they did decide to go ahead, they did so collectively. Given the risks involved and the amount of coverage required, it was impossible for individual companies to provide insurance on their own.

Nuclear Insurance Pools

Pools Provide a Solution

Instead of being provided by individual companies, in each country where nuclear insurance is available, it is provided by a "pool", a group of companies who have joined together voluntarily on a co-insurance basis. The terms and conditions under which business is carried on in each pool is set forth in a pool management agreement. Except for the United States, where there are two pools, there is a single nuclear insurance pool for each country. At present, there are 28 nuclear insurance pools throughout the world, each operating under different constitutions and procedures, in accordance with local legal, economic, social and market conditions. Since their creation, the capacity of the pools has increased many times over, as more companies join, and with experience they are willing to take more risks. For example, in France capacity increased from 7 million francs in 1957 to 157 million in 1987.

In some countries, such as the United Kingdom, the United States, Brazil, Canada, Japan, Korea and South Africa (and in Taiwan) the pool issues a policy in its own name and collects the premiums, which are subsequently distributed to the member companies. In others, where pools have no legal right to transact their own business, such as in continental Europe, a "fronting company" will issue the policy in its name on behalf of the pool. In the latter case, the fronting company collects the premiums and would handle the claims, should an accident occur.

In all the pools, participation is on a net-line retention basis. Each year, each member declares the amount of risk it is willing to accept for in each category or class of business: material damage, third party liability and reinsurance for foreign pools. These amounts are the member's subscription or *retention*. When the retentions of all the members are added up, then each company is assigned a percent of the total retention of the pool, which then becomes the percentage of the total premiums to which it is entitled and the percentage of the total expenses and claims it will have to pay. The sum of the subscription amounts of all the members is referred to as the total capacity for that particular pool.

Each company is responsible for its own share of the business and is not permitted to reinsure its retention individually, for if individual reinsurance were permitted, members might find themselves unwittingly reinsuring the same risk, thus facing a double exposure. This is possible, because reinsurance is usually conducted on the basis of "closed" portfolios of whose contents the reinsurer is unaware. If individual reinsurance is forbidden, then transparency is ensured. The members know precisely what their risk will be; there is no possibility of its being unexpectedly increased due to additional commitments through unknown channels.

Reinsurance is transacted by the pool as a whole. This is called "common account reinsurance". The consequence of this transparency has resulted in a greater commitment of the companies involved to nuclear risks than would be the case if they felt some uncertainty as to their total exposure if an accident should occur. In some cases, this commitment is considerably greater than that made in relation to other industrial risks. Furthermore , the pooling system has led to a reduction in costs on both the national and the international level.

The first pools were organised in the United States and Sweden in 1956. The following year, pools were also organised in Belgium, Denmark, Finland, France, Germany, Italy, Norway Switzerland and the United Kingdom. In 1958, Canada and the Netherlands joined the "club".

The International Pooling System

Due to the amounts insured and the relatively small capacity of the national pools, the total capacity of each pools is less than the amount usually required to be covered. Consequently, the national pools have to go to other pools for the balance. In the case of a large nuclear risk, the pool issuing the policy, or "ceding" pool, may have to rely on the entire world capacity for reinsurance. For example, the American pools have to reinsure 72 % of the amounts required under their policy limits. In fact, even the total world capacity is insufficient to meet the requirement for financial security in certain countries, so that different arrangements have to be made. (See the section on Germany in Chapter V). Thus, the different national pools rely heavily upon each other for support and international co-operation is essential.

Sources of Capacity for Reinsurance on the American Market in 1992

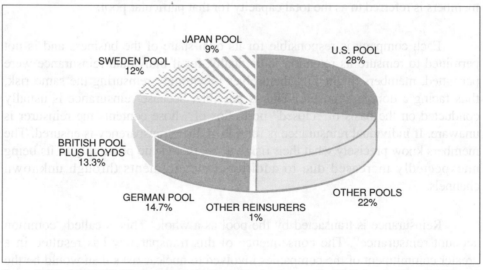

Source: J.Michael O'Connell, "Current Operating Practices of Nuclear Insurance Pools", *Nuclear Accidents, Liabilities and Guarantees*, Proceedings of the Helsinki Symposium, OECD, 1993.

The procedure is for the sponsoring pool to commit itself to provide the full amount of insurance to the policy holder, and then to reinsure most of that amount through reinsurance contracts with the other pools. Nevertheless, the pool issuing the policy (ceding pool) remains responsible for the total amount *vis-à-vis* the policy holder. Therefore, if an accident should occur and some of the reinsurance is uncollectable, the members of the sponsoring pool would have to pay more than their subscribed shares. As a result, the members of a pool frequently are liable for up to ten times their net subscription amounts.

34

Thus, the pools reinsure each other, most at the same time issuing policies on their domestic market and reinsuring abroad beyond their net capacity, while taking on foreign risks themselves by reinsuring pools in other countries. However, some pools exist only for the purpose of reinsurance. In some countries with no nuclear programmes, insurance companies will join together in a pool to provide reinsurance for the ceding pools.

Reinsurance is organised by means of reinsurance contracts between the ceding and the reinsuring pools. Although most pools follow more or less the same practices related to items such as procedures for the payment of premiums, losses and expenses, which are set forth in a reinsurance cover note, the American, and to a certain extent the Japanese pool, operate somewhat differently, transferring business on the basis of a formal agreement. Obviously, the entire system is based upon mutual confidence and a full exchange of information among the pools as to their constitutions and their mode of operation.

This confidence has been created by over three decades of close co-operation, consultation and sharing of information. The first reinsurance contracts were concluded with the establishment of the first pools and the first international conference on nuclear insurance took place in 1957 in London. Since then, international meetings and conferences, including the triennial London Conferences of Pool chairmen and the annual meetings of pool managers, have enabled the nuclear insurance industry to discuss common problems and to harmonise policies and procedures on a myriad of issues.

On the European level, since 1955, co-operation has been carried out through la Commission générale d'assurance des risques atomiques (CGARA) of le Comité européen des assurances (CEA). In order to promote the development of nuclear insurance and to represent the interests of nuclear insurers with international organisations, the Commission, which is comprised of national insurance associations which are members of the CEA, studies the problems posed by nuclear insurance, collects and distributes relevant information and documentation.

Coverage and Capacity

The pools generally provide coverage for both third party liability and property damage. In addition to nuclear power plants, which form the major part of their business, the pools also insure nuclear fuel fabrication plants, research reactors, plants for conditioning nuclear waste, reprocessing plants, nuclear waste facilities up to the time of closure (see Chapter VI) and transporters and suppliers of nuclear fuel and equipment.

In relation to third party liability, the coverage provided and the terms of the contract generally conform to the requirements of the national nuclear legislation, as the operators' financial security has to be approved by the responsible authorities. If the country concerned is a party to one of the liability conventions, then the legislation will incorporate or reflect its provisions. In many countries, the holding of an approved insurance contract is a pre-requisite for the issuance of a licence for a nuclear installation.

Nuclear Insurance Policies

Liability coverage

Fixed Installations

As already noted, the terms of a nuclear insurance policy will have to conform to the national law on liability for nuclear damage. It will also have to conform to the national law on insurance. For, nuclear insurance policies, whether for material damage or third party liability, are based upon conventional policies, with the addition of special terms responding to the specific exigencies of nuclear activities. The following is a summary of the special features of insurance policies for nuclear third party liability.

The policy will cover the third party liability of the operator of a nuclear installation in respect of damage caused by an accident in his installation or by nuclear material for which he is responsible. The liability covered will be that imposed by the national law. Policies are usually issued for only one year and payment will be made only for the consequences of the accident accruing while the policy is in force. Compensation will be provided only in the case of claims made by the victims within ten years of the date of the accident and within two or three years of the discovery of the damage, according to the legal time limit.

With a few exceptions, the amount of the policy will generally be somewhat above the legal liability limit. This latter feature is necessary to provide a partial reinStatement of coverage after an accident, because unlike the conventions, which provide for a limit per accident, insurance policies will provide for a limit during the lifetime of the policy (usually one year), or even of the installation (the United Kingdom, for example). In other words, there is no automatic re-inStatement of cover following payment of a claim and each claim paid diminishes the amount of indemnity available for the balance of the policy period. The purpose of this restriction is to ensure that each pool member's maximum commitment per risk and per year cannot be exceeded.

Because of the magnitude and the nature of the damage likely to be caused by a nuclear accident, it may be difficult to distinguish between nuclear damage and conventional damage. Consequently, as envisaged in the liability conventions, nuclear insurance policies will cover both nuclear and conventional damage when these are caused together by the same accident. Because it is more convenient for one policy to cover all risks related to a single installation, strictly non-nuclear damage will often also be covered, but in a separate section and for a separate amount, so as not to interfere with the operations of the nuclear liability law and the international conventions.

In accordance with usual practice, the policy will not cover damage due to armed conflict, acts of war, etc., nor to grave natural disasters in countries where these are frequent. On the other hand, accidents due to grave natural disasters may be covered in countries where they are infrequent. If legislation provides for liability in the case of damage caused by a grave natural disaster and it is excluded from the insurance policy, the State will invariably compensate the victims. Riots and civil commotions and terrorist acts may or may not be excluded. Always excluded from coverage will be damage caused by nuclear explosives (tests) and nuclear armaments.

Even though legally the operator may be liable for damage resulting from a deliberate release of radioactive material, compensation will not be provided by the nuclear insurance pool. If such liability is required to be covered by law, the policy will provide for recovery of the amount from the operator.

The Transport of Nuclear Materials

The operator of a nuclear installation is liable for any damage caused by nuclear materials for which he is responsible even in the course of transport, until another operator takes charge of them or liability is transferred by contract. In a few countries, notably Switzerland, the United Kingdom and the United States, liability for transport *within* the installation State is included in the operator's installation insurance. However, in most countries, liability for damage in the course of transport of nuclear materials, whether national or international, is provided in a separate policy.

Depending on the frequency of transports, the operator may chose to take out a separate policy for each trip or to conclude an agreement for insurance covering all transports within a specific period, generally one year. The operator will report all transports during the relevant period and the insurer will provide coverage for all of them. Obviously, the latter arrangement will save a good deal of time and trouble in the case of multiple transports. While in most countries, nuclear transport insurance is provided by the pools, in a few, it is provided by conventional insurers.

Although under the conventions and national legislation, the operator is required to hold a certain amount of financial security per accident, the insurers will only provide coverage per transport. In this way, they can control the precise amount of their exposure, even if there are several accidents in the course of one transport (however unlikely that may appear). Nevertheless, the amount insured will be slightly higher than the amount of the operator's legal liability, in order to furnish some protection for the remainder of a transport after an accident has occurred. In some countries, the law stipulates different liability amounts in accordance with the type of material being transported.

The special feature of liability for the transport of nuclear material is that if the transport is effected through several countries, it will be subject to several different legislative requirements. If all the States concerned are parties to the same convention, the laws involved should be quite similar. Furthermore, only one State will have jurisdiction and the operator's national law will determine certain factors such as the operator's liability limit. Similarly, if the transport is effected on the high seas, there should be no problem, as the operator's national law will apply.

On the other hand, if the transport involves a State party to one of the conventions and one or more States that are not parties, then considerable legal and practical complications may arise. If the installation State is party to one of the conventions, then the liability of the operator would arise under the convention in respect of an accident or damage occurring in another State party to that convention. Consequently, the rules of that convention would apply and the proceeds of the insurance policy could only be applied to the compensation of victims in the convention States.

At the same time, however, the operator might be held liable under the legislation of a country not party to the convention. To provide for compensation in such an eventuality, the operator might take out additional insurance, to cover liability under legislation not related to the conventions. If this is done, his national law will require to protect the insurance due in accordance with the convention. In such a situation the cover may be provided in one of two ways. First, the insurer could issue two separate policies insuring separate amounts, with one policy covering liability under national law or the law of another State party and the other liability under any other applicable legislation. Second, the insurer could issue a joint policy giving the victims subject to the law of a State party the right to claim up to the operator's liability limit under national law, with the balance going to the other victims.

Property damage coverage

This chapter is of course most concerned with liability insurance, but property damage cover is also important for those affected by the aftermath of a nuclear accident. In particular, it is the latter type of policy that will pay for decontamination of a site following an accident.

The most important type of property insurance provided by the nuclear pools is material damage cover for the installation and site. This includes the usual risks covered by conventional fire insurance, but also damage due to specific nuclear hazards such as uncontrolled reactivity (accidental chain reactions, overheating of a reactor) and accidental contamination by radioactive materials. Because it can be extremely difficult to distinguish between damage caused by nuclear perils and that caused by non-nuclear perils in the course of the same accident, the cover offered by the pools cannot be restricted to only one of the two categories.

As a matter of course, equipment is covered up to its insured value for radioactive contamination. However, the cost of decontamination can often exceed that value, so an additional cost item is often included in the policy, either for a special limit or up to the overall limit of cover for the installation. Special attention is paid to the cost of removing radioactive debris. In some markets, some cover is also available to pay for the removal of undamaged equipment if an installation is finally shut down following a major accident.

In the U.S.A., property insurance of reactor sites is compulsory, and by law the proceeds of the policy must be used first for stabilising, making safe and decontaminating the site, before any is applied to compensate loss of value of the installation.

In some markets coverage for machinery breakdown is included with material damage cover; in others a special policy is used; while in yet others it is covered by conventional insurance rather than by the nuclear pool. A material damage policy may also include consequential loss and loss of profits suffered by the operator, but this type of loss is usually covered by a separate contract, although often subject to a financial limit jointly with the property damage policy.

Physical damage coverage for nuclear equipment and material in the course of transport is not normally provided by the nuclear pools, and is instead dealt with by conventional insurance.

Chapter IV

THE INTERNATIONAL CONVENTIONS

Introduction

In the late 1950s, countries wishing to promote a nuclear power industry adopted legislation providing for third party liability in the field of nuclear energy. Among the earliest were the United States (1957), the Federal Republic of Germany, Switzerland and the United Kingdom (1959). At the same time, the liability issue was being discussed at the various international organisations responsible for the peaceful uses of nuclear energy: first, at the Organisation for European Economic Co-operation (later to become the OECD), but also at the International Atomic Energy Agency (IAEA) and the European Atomic Energy Community (Euratom). Since a nuclear accident might have transboundary consequences, States with nuclear power programmes recognised the need to conclude an international agreement that would govern compensation for damage both domestically and transnationally.

An international agreement was required to harmonise national laws in certain respects and to establish rules for cross-border legal actions against the nuclear operator by victims in other countries. Harmonization would create legal certainty, eliminate the possibility of discrimination, and ensure that claimants in States party to the convention would have their actions adjudged by similar laws irrespective of the location of the accident or the damage. An international agreement was also needed to govern questions of liability when nuclear materials were transported across international boundaries, from one country to another and through a third country.

For potential victims, it was extremely important to devise a special regime derogating from the general rules of private international law, as these would be inadequate for claiming compensation for transboundary nuclear damage. Under the general law, issues such as which courts have jurisdiction (which court should hear the case) and which law should apply can be extremely difficult to resolve. The laws regarding these matters can vary considerably in different national legal systems. For example, without a rule determining jurisdiction, claims for damages in relation to a single accident could be instituted in the courts of several countries, with different results in each. Furthermore, even if a victim did manage to win a judgement in his favour, he could face further obstacles in trying to execute it (obtain payment) if the assets of the operator are situated in another country, as the courts of one country do not automatically recognise the judgements of another.

The OECD Nuclear Energy Agency

The Nuclear Energy Agency (NEA) is a specialised body within the Organisation for Economic Co-operation and Development (OECD) created in 1958 by a decision of the Council of the Organisation. The NEA includes all members of the OECD except New Zealand, plus the Republic of Korea, which joined in 1993. The primary objective of the NEA is to promote co-operation among its members in furthering the development of nuclear power as a safe, environmentally acceptable and economic energy source, and its purpose is, *inter alia*, to:

- contribute to the promotion, by the responsible national authorities, of the protection of workers and the public against the hazards of ionising radiations and of the protection of the environment,

- contribute to the promotion of the safety of nuclear installations and materials by the responsible national authorities,

- contribute to the promotion of a system of third party liability and insurance with respect to nuclear damage.

The governing body of the NEA is the Steering Committee for Nuclear Energy. The Steering Committee has the power to promulgate decisions (which are legally binding) and recommendations with regard to the *Paris Convention on Nuclear Third Party Liability*.

Within a few years, two main conventions were adopted on civil liability in the nuclear field. On 29 July 1960, the *Paris Convention on Third Party Liability in the Field of Nuclear Energy* was adopted under the auspices of the then OEEC (later OECD). Three years later, the *Vienna Convention on Civil Liability for Nuclear Damage* was adopted under the auspices of the International Atomic Energy Agency. Also in 1963, some of the signatories of the *Paris Convention* adopted the *Brussels Convention Supplementary to the Paris Convention* to provide State funding for compensation above the liability of the operator.

The International Atomic Energy Agency

The International Atomic Energy Agency (IAEA) is an autonomous agency of potentially universal membership associated with the United Nations system. It was created in 1957 and in 1994 had 121 Member States from all parts of the world. According to its Statute, the Agency's two main objectives are to "accelerate and enlarge the contribution of atomic energy to peace, health and prosperity throughout the world", and to verify that nuclear materials and facilities under its safeguards are not used to "further any military purpose". Included in the first objective is the responsibility for establishing health and safety standards in order to protect health and to minimise danger to life and property. Over the years, the IAEA has sponsored a number of conventions relating to the peaceful uses of nuclear energy, including safety, emergency response and liability for nuclear damage.

The European Atomic Energy Community

As part of the European Union, EURATOM is one of the original components of the European Communities, along with the European Economic Community (EEC) and the European Coal and Steel Community (ECSC). EURATOM was created by a treaty signed in Rome in 1957 at the same time as the *EEC Treaty*. Its members are: Belgium, Denmark, France, Germany, Greece, Ireland, Italy, Luxembourg, the Netherlands, Portugal, Spain and the United Kingdom. The objective of EURATOM was to create a framework within which a powerful European nuclear industry could be established and flourish. In pursuing this goal, EURATOM fosters research, sets safety standards and develops relations with other competent organisations.

EURATOM members are also members of the other two organisations and NEA members are also members of the IAEA.

While the *Paris* and *Brussels Conventions* have, *de facto*, a regional vocation – all the parties being countries of western Europe – the *Vienna Convention* is of potentially universal membership. Originally, it was intended that the *Paris Convention* would create a special regime, together with the *Brussels Convention* on supplementary funding, applicable only to OECD countries, while the *Vienna Convention* would create a slightly different, general regime applicable world-wide, to which *Paris Convention* States could also adhere. In the event, since the *Paris Convention* parties had their own regime among like-minded States in the same geographic area, they did not perceive any need to become parties to the *Vienna Convention* as well. Furthermore, they concluded that because of the inconsistencies between the two conventions, a State could not be party to both of them. After the accident at Chernobyl, the States parties to both the *Paris* and the *Vienna Conventions* adopted a *Joint Protocol* to create a link between the two instruments. The *Joint Protocol* is discussed in Chapter VI.

Both civil liability conventions provide for private actions in the regular courts by victims of a nuclear accident to recover compensation for damage from the operator of the nuclear installation responsible for the accident. Actions (lawsuits) may be instituted by victims in any STATE party to the Convention. The basic features of the two conventions are:

– exclusive liability "channelled" to the operator of the nuclear installation involved;

– "absolute" or "strict" liability, with few exonerations;

– limitations on the amount of liability;

– limitations in time for the submission of claims;

– compulsory financial security;

– unity of jurisdiction;

– judgements enforceable in any of the States parties; and

– special rules for accidents during the transport of nuclear materials.

The conventions have a two-fold purpose: first, they share the basic aims of nuclear liability law in general, discussed in the previous chapter; second, they create a special regime of legal rules to facilitate litigation to claim compensation by the victims of nuclear accidents in foreign countries. In the preamble to the *Paris Convention*, the signatories declare themselves as being:

Desirous of ensuring adequate and equitable compensation for persons who suffer damage caused by nuclear incidents whilst taking the necessary steps to ensure that the development of the production and uses of nuclear energy for peaceful purposes is not thereby hindered...

The Paris-Brussels System

The Paris-Brussels system consists of two conventions, the *Paris Convention on Third Party Liability in the Field of Nuclear Energy* and the *Brussels Convention Supplementary to the Paris Convention*. The *Paris Convention* provides compensation for nuclear damage from the operator of the installation responsible for an accident. Should the operator's financial security prove insufficient to cover all the damage, the *Brussels Convention* provides two additional tiers of funding, from the installation State and from all the other States party to the Convention.

The Paris Convention on Third Party Liability
in the Field of Nuclear Energy

As noted above, the *Paris Convention* was adopted in 1960 under the auspices of the OECD/NEA. In 1964 a protocol was adopted that partly harmonised its provisions with those of the *Vienna Convention*. In 1982, yet another protocol changed the unit of account to the Special Drawing Right of the International Monetary Fund (SDR) and made some minor technical improvements.

The *Paris Convention* is open to all Member countries of the OECD by simple accession and to any other State by the unanimous consent of all States parties. At the present, it is essentially a European convention, as the non-European members of the NEA (Australia, Canada, Japan, Korea, Mexico and the United States) are not parties. Of the original 16 signatories, 13 have ratified the Convention, with Finland acceding in 1972, a year after it came into force. The 14 States parties are: Belgium, Denmark, Finland, France, Germany, Greece, Italy, the Netherlands, Norway, Portugal, Spain, Sweden, Turkey and the United Kingdom.

Parties to the *Paris Convention*

Signatories	Date of Ratification or Accession		
	Convention	1964 Protocol	1982 Protocol
Austria	—	—	—
Belgium	3 August 1966	3 August 1966	9 September 1985
Denmark	4 September 1974	4 September 1974	16 May 1989
Finland (acc.)	16 June 1972	16 June 1972	22 December 1989
France	9 March 1966	9 March 1966	6 July 1990
Germany	30 September 1975	30 September 1975	25 September 1985
Greece	12 May 1970	12 May 1970	30 May 1988
Italy	17 September 1975	17 September 1975	28 June 1985
Luxembourg	—	—	—
Netherlands	28 December 1979	28 December 1979	1 August 1991
Norway	2 July 1973	2 July 1973	3 June 1986
Portugal	29 September 1977	29 September 1977	28 May 1984
Spain	31 October 1961	30 April 1965	7 October 1988
Sweden	1 April 1968	1 April 1968	8 March 1983
Switzerland	—	—	—
Turkey	10 October 1961	5 April 1968	21 January 1986
United Kingdom	23 February 1966	23 February 1966	19 August 1985
Entry into force	*1 April 1968*	*1 April 1968*	*7 October 1988*

Scope

The scope of the Convention is established by the definitions and the provisions on geographical coverage. To cover both minor and major occurrences, the Convention uses (in the English text only) the term "incident" rather than "accident". For the purposes of the Convention, a "nuclear incident" is any occurrence or series of occurrences having the same origin which causes damage arising either from the radioactive properties or a combination of radioactive properties with toxic, explosive, or other hazardous properties of nuclear fuel or radioactive products or waste, or from ionising radiations emitted by any source of radiation inside a nuclear installation. Not covered are certain substances with a low level of radioactivity bearing only a minor risk.

"Nuclear installation" means reactors other than those comprised in any means of transport; factories for the manufacture or processing of nuclear substances; factories for the separation of isotopes of nuclear fuel; factories for the reprocessing of irradiated nuclear fuel; facilities for the storage of nuclear substances other than storage incidental to the carriage of such substances; and such other installations in which there are nuclear fuel or radioactive products or waste as determined by the Steering Committee for Nuclear Energy. The Steering Committee has exempted certain low-risk installations from the provisions of the Convention and has by a Decision determined that nuclear waste repositories are covered during their preclosure or operational phase, that is, while they are being filled and before they are permanently sealed.

The Convention does not apply to nuclear incidents occurring in the territory of non-contracting States or to damage suffered in such territory unless otherwise provided by the legislation of the installation State. However, in a Recommendation of 1968, the Steering Committee made clear that the Convention was applicable to nuclear incidents occurring on the high seas and to damage suffered on the high seas. In 1971 the Committee recommended that the scope of the *Paris Convention* be extended in national legislation to damage suffered in a contracting State, or on the high seas on board a ship registered in the territory of a contracting State even if the nuclear incident causing the damage has occurred in a non-contracting State. The purpose of this extension would be to provide compensation for victims in States parties if an operator in a State party is responsible, wherever an accident occurs.

Nature of Liability

The basic features of the *Paris Convention* are those listed in the introduction to this chapter. First, "strict" and "exclusive" liability is channelled to the operator of the nuclear installation where are held, or whence have come, or where are destined, the nuclear substances that caused the damage. As explained in a previous chapter, "strict" liability means that no fault or negligence on the part of the operator need be proven by the claimant and that there are few exonerations. Accordingly, under the Convention, the operator is liable for the damage indicated "upon proof that such damage or loss [...] was caused by a nuclear incident in such installation or involving nuclear substances coming from such installation..." In other words, the claimant need simply prove that he has suffered damage or injury and that the damage or injury was caused by the specific nuclear incident. This is a considerable advantage for the victim, as fault or negligence may be very difficult to prove.

47

Person Liable

For the purposes of the Convention, the "operator" of a nuclear installation is the person recognised or designated as the operator by the competent public authority. If the substances are in an installation at the time of an accident, then the operator of that installation is liable to compensate the damage thereby caused. If the radioactive substances involved in the accident have been in more than one nuclear installation, and are in a nuclear installation at the time the damage was caused, then it is the operator of the last installation who is liable. However, where the damage is caused by substances which are in a nuclear installation only temporarily for storage during the course of carriage, then the operator liable is not that of the place of storage, but the operator liable during the course of carriage. The operator may not be held liable outside the terms of the Convention.

If the accident has occurred during the course of carriage, then the operator responsible is the sender, until the receiver has assumed responsibility in accordance with the express terms of a written contract or has taken charge of the substances. Where nuclear substances are being sent to a person in a State not party to the Convention, then the sender is liable until the substances are unloaded from the means of transport. Conversely, where substances are being sent from a person in a State not party to the Convention, to an operator in a State party with his written consent, the latter will be liable from the time the substances are loaded onto the means of transport. Thus, during the course of carriage, a *Paris Convention* operator will always be held liable. If the accident involves substances from several installations, then the operators are jointly and severally liable, but the maximum total is the highest liability limit for which any one of them is liable, provided that no operator is required to pay more than the maximum for which he is personally liable.

The liability of the operator is "exclusive". This means that no one else may be held responsible. A supplier or contractor may not be held liable, even if he has been negligent or is at fault, except if he has accepted liability by contract, in which case the operator has a right of recourse. The operator also has a right of recourse against an individual acting with intent to cause damage, who has caused the nuclear incident in question. Even in these cases, the operator remains exclusively liable *vis-à-vis* the victims. The Convention does not affect any rights under public health insurance, social security or workmen's compensation, or any system relating to occupational diseases under national law. If a victim is compensated under other legislation or is cared for under public health insurance, then the body that has expended the funds may, under some national legislation, have a right of recourse against the operator.

Finally, the Convention does not affect the application of any convention on liability in the field of international transport in force or concluded at the time of the Convention. Thus, previous transport conventions placing liability on the carrier are still applicable. (See the section on Maritime Conventions, pp. 59-61, for an exception.)

Exonerations

Regarding exonerations, under the Convention, the operator is not liable for damage caused by a nuclear incident directly due to an act of armed conflict, hostilities, civil war, insurrection or, except in so far as the legislation of the installation State may provide to the contrary, a grave natural disaster of an exceptional character. A large number of States have taken advantage of the exception to hold the operator liable in the case of an accident due to a natural disaster, as they believe that the operator should foresee the possibility of such events and take the appropriate precautions.

Limitation in Amount of Liability

Liability is limited both in amount and in time. Pursuant to the *Paris Convention*, the maximum liability may not be greater than 15 million SDRs and not less than 5 million SDRs, although national legislation may fix a higher ceiling if financial cover is available. A contracting party may set a lower limit for less dangerous installations, of no less than 5 million SDRs, but must then provide public funds to cover liability up to the usual limit. If more than one operator is liable, then they are all jointly and severally liable.

The Special Drawing Right

The Special Drawing Right (SDR) is the unit of account used by the International Monetary Fund and is based upon a basket of weighted currencies. Because the original unit of account was based upon the official price of gold, which has since been abolished, the SDR was adopted to serve as the new unit to determine amounts of compensation. For the purposes of compensation, the amounts applicable in national legislation under the *Paris* and the *Brussels Conventions* are to be converted into national currency in accordance with the value established at the date of the incident. On 1 October 1994, the value of 1 SDR was US$ 1.4674.

In most contracting parties, the operator's liability is far higher than 15 million SDRs and in one, it is unlimited. In 1990, in order to promote *Harmonization* among the various national laws, the OECD Steering Committee for Nuclear Energy recommended that States parties raise their liability limits to at least 150 million SDRs, a sum that is well within the average available insurance capacity.

Limitation in Time

Because insurance is normally not available for more than ten years, the time limit for making claims is ten years from the date of the incident, with a possible exception under national law if measures have been taken by the installation State to cover the liability of the operator for actions instituted after the ten year limit. Further, the Convention permits States to establish in their national legislation a "discovery rule" providing that any claim must be made within a period of not less than two years from the time the victim discovered the damage and the identity of the operator. This latter period must still be within the general limit of ten years from the date of the accident.

In the case of damage caused by a nuclear accident involving nuclear substances that had been stolen, lost, jettisoned or abandoned, and not recovered, the time limit for making claims is 20 years from the date of the accident.

Financial Security

In order to ensure that funds will be available to pay compensation, the Convention States that the operator shall be required to have and maintain insurance or other financial security approved by the installation State for the amount of his liability established in accordance with the Convention. Although insurance is the most common form of financial security, it is possible also to furnish a bank guarantee, to pledge liquid assets, to establish a mutual fund or to benefit from a State guarantee or a form of indemnity or insurance provided by the State. The State will determine the terms and conditions for the financial security, which must be used only to compensate claims for damage under the Convention.

In the case of the international carriage of nuclear materials, the operator must provide the carrier with a certificate bearing the required information about his financial security. In 1967, the OECD Steering Committee for Nuclear Energy recommended a form of certificate to be used for carriage under the terms of the Convention. It contains the name and address of the operator, the type and duration of the financial guarantee, information about the substances being transported, and the itinerary covered by the guarantee.

The State is responsible for ensuring that the operator maintains the required financial security. As noted by the Exposé des motifs to the *Paris Convention*, if it does not, its international responsibility may be engaged.

Competent Court

The Convention provides that the right to compensation for damage caused by a nuclear incident may be exercised only against an operator liable in accordance with the Convention, or if such a right is provided under national law, against the insurer or other provider of a financial guarantee. The courts having jurisdiction are those where the nuclear incident occurred, except if the place of the incident cannot be determined or if the incident occurred outside the jurisdiction of any party. In case of doubt, the European Nuclear Energy Tribunal will determine which courts have jurisdiction.

The European Nuclear Energy Tribunal

The Tribunal was established pursuant to the 1957 *Convention on the Establishment of a Security Control in the Field of Nuclear Energy*. Although the security control has been suspended since 1976, the Tribunal retains its competence to settle disputes between States parties to the *Paris Convention* and the *Brussels Supplementary Convention*. It is comprised of seven independent judges appointed for a period of five years by the OECD Council.

Although the Convention provides for jurisdiction to lie with the courts of the installation State, it does not require that only one court have such jurisdiction. To facilitate consistency of decisions and the equitable distribution of compensation, in 1990 the Steering Committee recommended that parties designate a single court as the competent court.

The Applicable Law

The courts will apply the terms of the Convention as well as their own law in all matters not specifically covered by the Convention. Both the Convention and the national law must be applied without discrimination on the grounds of nationality, domicile or residence.

Compensation

The nature, form, and extent of the compensation, as well as its equitable distribution are governed by national law. The Convention provides that insurance premiums and monetary compensation are to be freely transferable between the parties, while judgements are to be enforceable in the territory of any contracting party. In cases against a State party, the State cannot invoke any jurisdictional immunities, except with respect to the execution of judgements. Costs and interest are additional to the liability amount.

Damage Covered

The operator is liable only for damage to or loss of life of any person, and damage to or loss of any property other than property on the site of the accident. The text of the *Paris Convention* does not mention compensation for preventive or protective measures or for damage to the environment. However, it is possible that the costs of preventive measures where an accident has occurred could be compensated under national law.

Additional Compensation

A State party may take any measures that it considers necessary to provide for an increase in the amount of the compensation specified in the Convention. Clearly, this refers to the possibility of providing public funds above the limitation of the liability of the operator, as is done in most States. It would also permit a system of operator pools to furnish additional compensation. In relation to the provision of public funds in excess of the minimum 5 million SDRs, States are entitled to apply any such measure in any form under conditions that may derogate from the provisions of the Convention. The *Brussels Convention* is an example of a collective use of this latter provision.

The Brussels Convention Supplementary to the Paris Convention of 29 July 1960 on Third Party Liability in the Field of Nuclear Energy.

Even before its adoption, States were aware that due to the limits on the operator's liability in the *Paris Convention*, not all of the damage from a nuclear accident could be compensated under its terms. Therefore, the six original members of the European Atomic Energy Community (EURATOM) explored the possibility of concluding another convention supplementary to the *Paris Convention* to provide additional funding by the States parties. After a draft was produced in 1962, the initiative passed to the NEA. Eventually, thirteen of the States which had signed the *Paris Convention* also signed the *Brussels Convention*. At present, there are 11 parties to the Convention.

Parties to the *Brussels Convention*

Signatories	Date of Ratification or Accession	
	Convention and 1964 Protocol	1982 Protocol
Austria	—	—
Belgium	20 August 1985	20 August 1985
Denmark	4 September 1974	10 May 1989
Finland (acc.)	14 January 1977	15 January 1990
France	30 March 1966	11 July 1990
Germany	1 October 1975	25 September 1985
Italy	3 February 1976	14 June 1985
Luxembourg	—	—
Netherlands	28 September 1979	1 August 1991
Norway	7 July 1973	13 May 1986
Spain	27 July 1966	29 September 1988
Sweden	3 April 1968	22 March 1983
Switzerland	—	—
United Kingdom	24 March 1966	8 August 1985
Entry into force	*4 December 1974*	*1 August 1991*

Like the *Paris Convention*, the *Brussels Convention* was also amended by Protocols adopted in 1964 and 1982. In addition to changing the unit of account to the SDR, the *1982 Protocol* also raised the amount of compensation available. Since the cumulative effect of inflation over two decades had seriously eroded the original amounts, they were increased by a factor of 2.5, so the total amount of compensation under Paris plus Brussels went from 120 million units of account to 300 million SDRs. The 1982 revision came into force in 1991.

The scope of the *Brussels Convention* is limited to damage caused by nuclear accidents other than those occurring entirely in the territory of a non-contracting State. The incident must be one for which an operator would be liable under the *Paris Convention* and the courts of a contracting party must have jurisdiction. Within these parameters, the Convention applies to damage suffered:

– in the territory of a contracting party;

– on or over the high seas on board a ship or aircraft registered in the territory of a contracting party; or

– on or over the high seas by a national of a contracting party provided that, in the case of damage to a ship or an aircraft, the ship or aircraft is registered in the territory of a contracting party.

In this Convention, the term "national" includes a contracting party, any of its subdivisions and any public or private body whether corporate or not. Further, a State may choose to assimilate foreigners resident on its territory to nationals.

The *Brussels Convention* establishes a three-tiered compensation system. At the first level, compensation is provided by the insurance or other financial security of the operator up to the maximum of liability set by national law in accordance with the provisions of the *Paris Convention*. In the second tier, the balance between this amount and 175 million SDRs is then provided by the government in which the nuclear installation of the operator liable is situated (the installation State). The remaining amount, if there is any damage left uncompensated, between 175 million and 300 million SDRs is contributed jointly by all the States parties according to a special formula derived from the gross national product (GNP) and the thermal nuclear power capacity of the reactors situated in each State.

Operation of the *Brussels Convention*
Tiers of Compensation

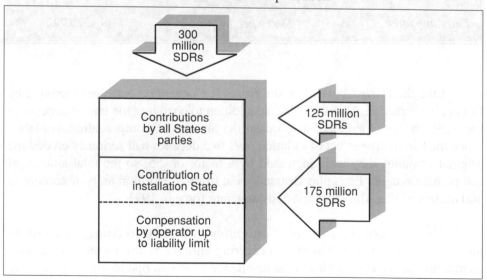

To implement the convention, parties may provide in their national law, either that the operator is liable up to 300 million SDRs, or that the maximum is some other amount, not less than 5 million SDRs, and that the balance between that amount and 300 million SDRs shall be provided by some other means. If there is a nuclear accident in a State party to the *Brussels Convention* and the damage exceeds the limit of the operator's liability, then the installation State would contribute funds to the compensation of the victims for any amount between the liability limit and the equivalent of 175 million SDRs. If some damage still remains uncompensated, the rest of the States parties to the Convention will contribute funds proportionately, in accordance with their pre-determined share, up to the maximum limit of 300 million SDRs.

Under the terms of the *Brussels Convention*, victims are entitled to full compensation for the damage suffered under national law, except that if the aggregate amount of liability exceeds the 300-million-SDR limit, any party may establish equitable criteria for apportionment. The court having jurisdiction will decide upon the system of disbursements. In calculating the public funds to be made available under the Convention, account will be taken only of claims made within the basic ten year limitation period. If a party has established a "discovery rule", as permitted under the *Paris Convention*, it must be three years from the date at which the victim had knowledge or should have had knowledge of both the damage and the operator liable. Judgements are enforceable in the territory of any party.

If a party uses the options in the *Paris Convention* to extend its territorial scope or to provide for liability in case of natural disaster, then the other parties cannot be required to provide the additional compensation necessary to meet the claims without their express consent. However, the parties may make provisions outside the scope of either the *Paris* or *Brussels Convention* provided that no obligation is involved from the other parties. Furthermore, any contracting party may conclude an agreement with a non-party concerning compensation out of public funds for damage caused by a nuclear accident.

Revisions, Decisions and Recommendations

As already indicated, the *Paris* and *Brussels Conventions* have been modified several times, twice by formal amendments, in 1964 and 1982, and a number of times by Decisions. In addition, a number of non-binding Recommendations on the interpretation and the application of the Conventions have been adopted. Since their inception, the Conventions have been kept under continuous review by the NEA Group of Governmental Experts on Nuclear Third Party Liability in the Field of Nuclear Energy. Periodically, the group makes proposals for decisions, recommendations or interpretations with a view to improving the operation of the Conventions. These proposals may then be formally adopted by either the OECD Council or the Steering Committee for Nuclear Energy.

Under the *Paris Convention*, the Steering Committee is empowered to make certain legally binding decisions in relation to the definitions of "nuclear installation" and "nuclear fuel", and in order to exempt any nuclear installations, fuel or substances from the scope of the Convention, if in its view the small extent of the risk so warrants. In addition, pursuant to its general powers under the NEA Statute, the Steering Committee may adopt recommendations or interpretations concerning the *Paris Convention* which are not legally binding. Similarly, the OECD Council, pursuant to its general powers under the *OECD Convention*, may adopt non-binding recommendations concerning both Conventions.

Lack of space precludes a discussion of all the decisions and recommendations, but some of them are referred to in the relevant passages of this study. The complete set of decisions, recommendations and interpretations up to 1990 are available in an OECD publication.

Here, it might be noted that two recommendations concerning the operation of the *Brussels Convention* were adopted by OECD Council in November 1992. First, in some *Paris Convention* States, the limit of the liability of the operator is higher than the 175-million-SDR limit set for the contributions of both the operator and the installation State in the *Brussels Convention*. Moreover, in a few, the limit is even above the *Brussels Convention* maximum of 300 million SDRs. Consequently, if the damage exceeded 175 or 300 million SDRs, the amount of collective State funding would be reduced or would not be available at all to compensate victims of accidents in those States.

In order to provide additional funding for the victims, the OECD Council recommended that each party issue a declaration stating that it would make available its share of public funds up to the cumulative limit of 125 million SDRs to the extent that the damage caused by a nuclear incident exceeded the amount of the operator's financial security. The second recommendation relates to the *Joint Protocol* and is discussed in Chapter VI.

The *Vienna Convention on Civil Liability for Nuclear Damage*

At the same time as the OECD/NEA was beginning work on the *Paris Convention*, the International Atomic Energy Agency (IAEA) had decided to prepare its own convention on the same topic. In May 1963, the members of the IAEA adopted the *Vienna Convention on Civil Liability for Nuclear Damage*. It came into force in 1977 and is potentially universal in scope, with accession open to all members of the United Nations, the specialised agencies and the IAEA. Up to the time of the accident at Chernobyl, the Convention had attracted only ten adherents, only two of which harboured functioning nuclear reactors. However, since the revision exercise currently underway, the number of States parties has almost doubled. The proposals to amend the *Vienna Convention* are described in Chapter VIII.

Parties to the *Vienna Convention*

Countries	Date of Ratification or Accession
Argentina	25 April 1967
Armenia (acc.)	24 August 1993
Bolivia (acc.)	10 April 1968
Brazil (acc.)	26 March 1993
Bulgaria	24 August 1994
Cameroon (acc.)	6 March 1964
Chile	23 November 1989
Croatia (succ.)	8 October 1991 (date of effect)
Cuba	25 October 1965
Czech Republic (acc.)	24 March 1994
Egypt	5 November 1965
Estonia (acc.)	9 May 1994
Hungary (acc.)	28 July 1989
Lithuania (acc.)	15 September 1992 (date of effect)
Macedonia (succ.)	8 September 1991 (date of effect)
Mexico (acc.)	25 April 1989
Niger (acc.)	24 July 1979
Peru (acc.)	26 August 1980
Philippines	15 November 1965
Poland (acc.)	23 January 1990
Romania (acc.)	29 December 1992
Slovenia (succ.)	25 June 1991 (date of effect)
Trinidad and Tobago (acc.)	31 January 1966
Yugoslavia	12 August 1977
Entry into force	*12 November 1977*

In its current text, the *Vienna Convention* is quite similar to the *Paris Convention*. Embodied are most of the same basic principles: private actions in the national courts; strict or absolute liability of the operator; channelling exclusive liability to the operator; compulsory financial security; limitation of liability; limitation in time for the submission of claims; special rules for transport cases; unity of jurisdiction; and reciprocal enforcement of judgements.

Yet, there are also deliberate differences between the two conventions, some of them significant. In general, the *Vienna Convention* contains fewer restrictions than the *Paris Convention* and is therefore more flexible. For example, in relation to the limitation of liability, the *Vienna Convention* stipulates only a minimum of 5 million dollars, with a maximum being permitted, if desired, in national legislation. Consequently, States are free to set whatever maximum they wish in their national legislation, or even to provide for unlimited liability. Furthermore, the amount of financial security to be provided by the operator is left to the discretion of the contracting party. In addition, Vienna is in certain respects more specific. For example, "nuclear damage" is defined and the operator's liability is explicitly stated to be absolute.

On the other hand, in some respects, it is less protective of the claimant, as it permits the operator to be relieved of his liability if the damage has resulted either wholly or in part from the gross negligence of the victim, and it allows the execution of judgements to be denied under certain conditions.

The following is an indication of the major differences between the two Conventions:

- geographical scope (Paris may be extended by a party to non-contracting States, while Vienna may not);

- limits of liability (in Vienna, there is no upper limit and the lower limits differ);

- definition of damage (in Vienna, the definition is open, i.e., the national legislation may include damage other than the personal injury and property damage provided for in Paris);

- State guarantee of payment of compensation in case of the failure of the operator's financial security (explicit in Vienna, not in Paris);

- rights of recourse (additional rights in Paris);

- amount of financial security for nuclear material in transit (in Paris, may be raised to national level);

- liability for damage resulting from ionising radiation from any source within a nuclear installation (included in Paris, but in Vienna only if in national law);

- liability for damage to the means of transport (included in Paris, optional in Vienna);

- designation of the competent court in case of uncertainty (under Paris, by the European Nuclear Energy Tribunal; under Vienna, by agreement);

- reciprocal enforcement of judgements in all States parties (in Vienna, may be denied for certain specified reasons);

- amendments and reservations (provisions in Paris, not Vienna);

- definitions (under Paris, the Steering Committee for Nuclear Energy may extend the definitions of the terms "nuclear fuels" and "nuclear installations" and may exclude certain nuclear fuels, installations and substances from the application of the Convention) (in Vienna, "nuclear damage" is defined); and

- dispute settlement (under Paris, disputes are to be submitted to the Steering Committee for Nuclear Energy, and then to the European Nuclear Energy Tribunal, while under Vienna there are no provisions in the Convention, but an Optional Protocol that is not in force);

- compulsory financial security (not required for States in Vienna).

The *Vienna Convention* has never been revised. Finally, unlike the *Paris Convention*, the *Vienna Convention* is not supplemented by another instrument providing for State funding in addition to the compensation paid by the operator.

The Maritime Conventions

The Convention Relating to Civil Liability in the Field of Maritime Carriage of Nuclear Material

As noted above, both the *Paris* and the *Vienna Convention*s preserved the application of previously concluded transport conventions. This meant that in the event of an accident involving the transportation of nuclear materials, the *Paris* or *Vienna Convention* and a transport convention not designed with nuclear activities in mind might be applicable simultaneously to the issue of third party liability. In particular, there were a number of maritime liability conventions that would apply to the carriage of nuclear materials by sea. If there were an accident involving nuclear materials for which an operator were liable under one of the nuclear liability conventions, and if the flag State of the vessel were party to a convention on maritime liability, then both conventions might be applicable. Thus, the owner of the vessel might be liable under the transport convention at the same time as the operator is liable under either the *Paris* or *Vienna Convention*, each with a separate liability limit. Furthermore, courts in different States might have jurisdiction over the accident.

Finally, because of the legal uncertainty, insurance companies were refusing to provide coverage of the maritime transport of nuclear materials. To avoid the resulting confusion and to remedy the lack of insurance coverage, after the coming into force of the *Paris Convention*, the responsible international organisations – the NEA, the IAEA and the International Maritime Organisation (IMO) – discussed the question of priorities in relation to the various conventions relevant to maritime transport. They decided to sponsor the conclusion of a new treaty to give priority to the *Paris* and *Vienna Convention*s.

The *Convention relating to Civil Liability in the Field of Maritime Carriage of Nuclear Material* was adopted in December 1971 and came into force on 15 July 1975. In November 1993, the parties were: Argentina, Belgium, Denmark, Finland, France, Gabon, Germany, Italy, Liberia, the Netherlands, Norway, Spain, Sweden and Yemen. In the preamble to the Convention, the purpose is declared as being to ensure that the operator of a nuclear installation will be exclusively liable for damage caused by a nuclear incident occurring in the course of maritime carriage of nuclear material.

This effect is achieved by providing in the Convention that any person who might be held liable for nuclear damage in the course of maritime carriage by virtue of an international convention or a national law, is exonerated from such liability if the operator of a nuclear installation is liable for such damage under either the *Paris* or the *Vienna Convention*, or under a national law governing nuclear liability, provided that the national law is in all respects as favourable to the victims as the *Paris* or the *Vienna Convention*. The exoneration also applies to damage to the nuclear installation or the means of transport for which the operator is not liable. However, it does not affect the liability of an individual who has caused the damage intentionally.

Similar exemption clauses have been included in most recent civil liability conventions covering activities where nuclear substances may be involved, including the 1989 convention on transport by road rail and inland waterways, and the just adopted *1993 Council of Europe Convention on Civil Liability concerning Activities Dangerous to the Environment*. These exclude, under certain conditions, damage caused by nuclear materials. Two other conventions now being negotiated, treating liability for damage caused during the carriage of hazardous substances by sea and the transport and disposal of hazardous waste, may also exclude nuclear materials. These are the IMO draft International Convention on Liability and Compensation for Damage in Connection with the Carriage of

Dangerous Goods by Sea and the *Liability Protocol to the Basel Convention on the Control of Transboundary Movements of Hazardous Wastes and their Disposal*. Nuclear materials may be excluded as liability resulting from their use or transport is already, or may be in future, covered by the conventions on nuclear liability.

The Convention on the Liability of Operators of Nuclear Ships

The *Convention on the Liability of Operators of Nuclear Ships* was adopted in Brussels on 25 May 1962, as a free-standing convention, not under the sponsorship of either the NEA or the IAEA. The Convention applies to nuclear damage caused by a nuclear incident occurring in any part of the world and involving the nuclear fuel of, or radioactive products or waste produced in, a nuclear ship flying the flag of a State party. The Convention is not in force, most likely for the three following reasons. First, as there are virtually no commercial nuclear ships in operation, and as there may never be, States do not see any point in ratifying it. Historically, whenever nuclear ships have wished to call at certain ports, special agreements covering liability were concluded between the port State and the flag State. Second, the Convention covers military vessels and the countries with major fleets of nuclear warships do not wish to become parties. Finally, liability is strictly limited to a single anachronistic amount: 1,500 million gold francs.

In most respects, the *Nuclear Ships Convention* closely resembles the *Paris* and *Vienna Conventions*, being somewhat closer to the Vienna one: civil liability, absolute liability of the operator, channelling, limitation of the amount of liability, limitation in time for the submission of claims, compulsory financial security, the exclusion of damage to the ship itself, exoneration with respect to damage caused intentionally by the victim, etc. However, the only exoneration is for damage directly due to an act of war, hostilities, civil war or insurrection. As in the *Vienna Convention*, any prescription period must be not less than three years and States and State agencies are not required to hold financial security. Finally, the licensing State is bound to compensate the victims up to the liability limit, if the operator's financial security fails.

On the other hand, in contrast to the conventions concerning land-based reactors, an action for compensation relating to nuclear ships may be brought, at the option of the claimant, either before the courts of the licensing State or before the courts of the contracting State(s) in whose territory nuclear damage has been sustained.

There are four parties to the *Nuclear Ships Convention*: Portugal, the Netherlands, Zaire and the Malagasy Republic.

Chapter V

NATIONAL REGIMES

The first national laws concerning liability for nuclear damage were adopted in the late 1950s just before the conclusion of the *Paris* and *Vienna Conventions*. Not surprisingly, most national laws are based upon the same fundamental principles as the Conventions. Not only were the Conventions influenced by the earlier national laws, but also both were inspired by the same concepts and drafted by some of the same people. After the adoption of the Conventions, national laws of the parties to the conventions had to conform to them, except for the optional provisions, where parties had some discretion. Finally, even national laws having no connection to the Conventions embody some of the same principles, especially that of the absolute liability of the operator and the requirement for financial security, simply because those principles were considered to be the most appropriate for the nuclear field.

On the other hand, there are some striking differences between the provisions of the conventions and the legislation of non-parties, as well as some interesting additions to the rules by some countries that are parties. Indeed, some of these different provisions have served as models for States proposing revisions to the existing conventions. In this chapter are examined a number of these national laws, chosen either because the countries involved have significant nuclear power programmes, because the legislation differs somewhat from the Conventions (or both), or because the legislation contains provisions similar to those being proposed for inclusion in the revised conventions. See Chapters VI and VII.

Canada

General

In 1993, Canada had 22 nuclear power plants. Although Canada is not a party to any of the nuclear liability conventions, its legislation is based upon some of the same principles. The relevant legislation is the *Act Respecting Civil Liability for Nuclear Damage (Nuclear Liability Act)*, as amended.

Scope

In general, an operator of a Canadian nuclear installation is not liable for any damage caused outside of Canada. Nevertheless, special arrangements may be made on the basis of reciprocity and such arrangements were concluded with the United States in 1976. Implementation is effected by the *Canada-United States Nuclear Liability Rules*, in force on 11 October 1976.

Nature of Liability

The nuclear operator is under a duty to ensure that no damage is caused by nuclear material under his control, either in his installation or during the course of carriage. A breach of this duty entails absolute and exclusive liability.

Exonerations

The operator is not liable for damage caused by an accident due to an act of war or to an intentional illegal act of the victim.

Amount of Liability

Although there is no provision expressly limiting the amount of liability, the same result is achieved by limiting the amount of financial security and by absolving the operator from responsibility if this limit is exceeded.

Damage Covered

Compensable damage includes loss of life and personal injury and loss of or damage to property, or damage resulting from such loss or damage.

Financial Security

The operator must maintain approved financial security for up to C$ 75 million (39.8 million SDRs). For basic amounts lesser than C$ 75 million, supplementary insurance must be obtained, with the Canadian government acting as reinsurer.

Time Limits

There is a three year discovery rule and an absolute limit of ten years from the date of the accident.

Competent Court

Actions must be brought before the court where the damage was suffered, or if this would create multiple jurisdiction, where the accident occurred.

State Intervention

There are special measures for compensation where the total claims are likely to exceed the amount of financial security, or where the government deems it to be in the public interest. A Proclamation is issued which halts any legal process and terminates any liability of the operator. The State then becomes liable to pay compensation to the victims and the operator to reimburse the State up to the limit of his financial security. For amounts greater than C$ 75 million, Parliament must appropriate the funds.

To adjudicate the claims and determine the amount of compensation, the government appoints a Nuclear Damage Claims Commission comprised of judges and lawyers. The Commission may take special measures to investigate the claims, including the use of experts and the examination of injury and damage. When required due to the distress or suffering of the victims, the government may provide interim financial assistance. It may also make regulations establishing priorities among the victims, or to exclude from compensation, temporarily or permanently, certain categories of damage, as well as to provide for payments by installment or *pro-rata* payments.

France

General

France has a substantial nuclear power programme, with 57 reactors having a total capacity of 59,000 MWe, and five more under construction. France is a party to both the *Paris* and *Brussels Conventions* and has signed, but not ratified, the *Joint Protocol*. In addition, it is party to the *Convention Relating to Civil Liability in the Field of Maritime Carriage of Nuclear Material*. Liability for nuclear damage is governed by the Act of 30 October 1968 on third party liability in the field of nuclear energy, as amended in 1990. In the Act, the obligatory provisions of the *Paris Convention* are taken as given, and only the questions permitting choices or options are addressed. As in the *Paris Convention*, the operator is absolutely and exclusively liable; the installations covered are the same; as are the rules for liability during transport and the requirement to hold financial security.

Exonerations

The operator is exonerated if the accident results directly from armed conflict or a grave natural disaster of exceptional character.

Amount of Liability

The maximum liability of the operator is 600 million francs (approximately 74.5 million SDRs) per nuclear incident in an installation and 150 million francs in the course of carriage. In the case of a minor risk in an installation, the amount may be reduced to 150 million francs. In the case of carriage, the State will pay compensation for any damage above the limit, in accordance with the *Brussels Convention*. However, if the carriage is not subject to the *Paris Convention*, the carrier must have a financial guarantee equivalent to 1,500 million francs, approximately the amount of the first tier of the *Brussels Convention*.

Military Installations

If an accident occurs in a military installation, compensation will be paid by the French State, up to a maximum of 2,500 million francs per incident, where the victim would have been entitled to invoke the *Brussels Convention* had the installation been used for peaceful purposes.

Damage and Compensation

Under French law, the concept of damage covers: expenses relating to personal injury as such (medical expenses, hospital expenses, disability payments,

payments to heirs of a deceased person); the cost of evacuating and lodging the local population and any resulting loss of salary; loss of production caused by contamination; clean-up costs (decontaminating property); and loss of income by neighbouring enterprises obliged to interrupt their activities.

Financial Security

Upon the proposal of the minister responsible for atomic energy, the Minister for Economic Affairs and Finance may provide a complete or partial State guarantee for operators of nuclear installations to take the place of insurance or other financial security. With a State guarantee, the Central Reinsurance Fund is empowered to cover the risks for which operators of nuclear installations are liable.

Time Limits

Actions (law suits) for compensation must be brought within ten years of the accident and three years of the discovery of the damage and the identity of the operator. Beyond the ten year limit, up to fifteen years from the date of the accident, the State will pay compensation for damage caused by accidents on French territory and for which a French court has jurisdiction under the *Paris Convention*.

Competent Court

Under the Act, only a single court has jurisdiction, the Tribunal de grande instance de Paris.

Priorities

If the funds available under the Act appear insufficient to compensate all the damage, the Council of Ministers will promulgate a decree establishing the conditions for distribution of the amount available. Priority is to be given to the payment of compensation for personal injury on terms similar to those applicable to industrial accidents, the balance being shared among the victims in proportion to any uncompensated personal injury and any damage to property, evaluated in accordance with the rules of ordinary law.

State Intervention

In addition to paying compensation for damage becoming apparent after the expiry of the time limit, the State will also compensate the victims up to the liability limit, in the event of a failure to pay by the operator or the financial security.

Germany

General

Germany has an important nuclear research and power programme, with 21 reactors currently in operation, for a total capacity of 22,550 MWe. It is party to the *Paris* and *Brussels Conventions*, has signed the *Joint Protocol* and is party to the *Convention on Maritime Carriage*. In Germany nuclear liability is governed by a section of the *Act on the Peaceful Uses of Nuclear Energy and Protection Against Its Hazards (Atomic Energy Act)* of 23 December 1959, as subsequently amended and supplemented by various ordinances. The *Atomic Energy Act* declares the *Paris Convention* to be directly applicable under German law and includes provisions relating to the options in the Convention. On the other hand, the *Brussels Convention* and the provisions on State intervention are not directly applicable.

Exonerations

In Germany, the operator of a nuclear installation is absolutely and exclusively liable for damage resulting from all accidents, even those caused by armed conflicts or natural disasters.

Amount of Liability

The liability of nuclear operators in Germany is unlimited. However, in the event of an accident directly caused by armed conflict or a natural disaster, liability is limited to the maximum of the State guarantee, at present DM 1,000 million (432.9 million SDRs). In the event of damage occurring in other States, the maximum amount of compensation available is subject to reciprocity; that is, it will be paid only if the other State has established an equivalent system in relation to Germany. In the case of parties to the *Brussels Convention*, this provision applies to amounts over the 300 million SDR limit, while in other States (including parties to the *Paris Convention* only), reciprocity applies to compensation above 15 million SDRs.

In 1986, Germany concluded a liability agreement with Switzerland providing for full reciprocity. Swiss operators also have unlimited liability.

Damage and Compensation

The damage covered is generally the same as that in the *Paris Convention*.

Financial Security

In the case of installations whose liability is governed by the *Paris Convention*, the financial security must be in due proportion to the hazards involved. In general, it must equal the amount of insurance available on the market at reasonable rates, up to a maximum of DM 500 million (216.5 million SDRs). Although the Federal government and the States (Länder) are not required to hold financial security, the latter must provide a guarantee acceptable to the licensing authority. In the case of carriage, the financial guarantee must not exceed DM 50 million. However, there are special provisions regarding countries party to the *Paris Convention* who are not also party to the *Brussels Convention*.

In Germany, the financial security of operators of nuclear power plants is provided in two tiers, with the operators acting as their own reinsurers for the second tier. In the first tier, up to DM 200 million is provided by ordinary third party liability insurance. For the remaining amount, all the operators have joined together in a co-operative partnership which has concluded a contract with the six leading German insurance companies to provide up to DM 300 million. The operators pay an advance fee calculated on the basis of their nominal thermal power and a deferred premium if compensation has to be paid between DM 200 and 500 million.

Time Limits

Claims must be submitted within three years after the discovery of the damage and the identity of the operator and 30 years after the date of the accident.

Competent Court and Applicable Law

Under German law, several courts may have jurisdiction concurrently: the place where the accident occurred, where the damage was suffered, or where the operator has his place of residence (which may not be the place where the installation is situated. If a German court has jurisdiction, German law will apply, with some exceptions.

State Intervention

If the liability of the operator is not covered or cannot be satisfied by his financial security, the State will indemnify him up to an amount that is twice his financial security. At present, that is a maximum of DM 1,000 million. As well as the insolvency of the insurer or financial guarantor or the insufficiency of the amount, this indemnity covers such uninsurable risks as accidents caused by armed conflict and damage arising more than ten years after the accident. The State may take recourse against the operator thus indemnified if: 1) he has not complied with the instructions of the competent authorities; 2) he or his legal representative has caused the damage wilfully or by gross negligence; 3) compensation has been paid because the financial security did not correspond to the determination by the competent authority.

In the case of nuclear damage suffered in Germany for which a foreign operator is liable, the State will pay up to the maximum amount of indemnification, if the victims cannot obtain compensation under the law of a State party to the *Paris Convention* for certain listed reasons, or if an applicable foreign law or international agreement provides for compensation less than that obtainable under the *Atomic Energy Act*. These provisions are applicable irrespective of nationality, except that for foreign victims who are not habitual residents of Germany, they are applicable only in the case of reciprocity. Compensation for damage caused by the accident at Chernobyl was provided under the provisions of the *Atomic Energy Act* concerning accidents occurring in other States.

Japan

General

Japan has 48 nuclear power plants in operation and six under construction. Japan is not a party to any of the nuclear liability conventions. Liability for nuclear damage is governed by *Law No. 147 of 17 June 1961 on Compensation for Nuclear Damage* as last amended on 31 March 1989 (the *Compensation Law*); the Ordinance for the Enforcement of the Compensation Law, Cabinet Order No. 44 of 6 March 1962 as last amended on 17 November 1989; and *Law No. 148 of 17 June 1961 on Indemnity Agreements for Compensation of Nuclear Damage* as last amended on 27 May 1988 (the *Indemnity Law*).

Scope

The Japanese law contains no special provisions on geographic coverage. Compensation is provided for nuclear damage caused by the operation of nuclear installations, the transport and storage of nuclear materials and the disposal of radioactive waste. In the legislation, the term "reactor operation etc." is used to define these activities.

Nature of Liability

The operator responsible for the activity causing nuclear damage is absolutely and exclusively liable.

Transport

When nuclear damage results from the transport of nuclear fuel, the operator sending the material is liable, unless there is a written agreement to the contrary. In the case of a shipment between a Japanese operator and a foreign operator, the Japanese operator is liable.

Damage Covered

The Law defines nuclear damage as any damage caused by the effects of the nuclear fission process of nuclear fuel, by the effects of radiation of nuclear fuel material, or by the toxic nature of such materials.

Financial Security

A nuclear operator must maintain financial security for the amount of ¥30 billion (150 million SDRs), in the form of insurance, a deposit or an equivalent arrangement for the compensation of nuclear damage for each single site, as approved by the authorities. Lower amounts are established for lower risks.

Time Limits

Claims must be submitted within ten years of the date of the incident.

Competent Court and Procedure

The general provisions of the civil law apply; however, a Dispute Reconciliation Committee for Nuclear Damage Compensation may be established as an organisation attached to the Science and Technology Agency to mediate disputes.

State Intervention

First, operators covering their liability by insurance must in addition conclude an indemnity agreement with the government for the compensation of

71

nuclear damage not covered by the insurance contract and other security. For this indemnity, the operator pays a fee. The government will indemnify the operator for compensation paid in respect of:

a)   nuclear damage caused by an earthquake or volcanic eruption;

b)   nuclear damage caused by an unknown occurrence during normal operation; and

c)   nuclear damage otherwise covered, but for which compensation is claimed after the ten year limit, for a justifiable reason.

Second, the government will assist the operator to compensate the damage, when the amount required exceeds the financial security and such assistance is deemed necessary to fulfill the purpose of the Compensation Law. If the damage is caused by a natural disaster or an insurrection, the government will take the necessary measures to relieve the victims and to prevent any increase of the damage.

Netherlands

General

The Netherlands has two nuclear power plants with a total of 504 MWe. It is party to the *Paris Convention*, the *Brussels Convention*, the *Joint Protocol* and the *Convention on the Maritime Carriage of Nuclear Material*. Liability for nuclear damage is governed by the *Nuclear Incidents (Third Party Liability) Act* of 1979, as amended, most recently in 1991. The *Liability Act* takes the basic provisions of the *Paris* and *Brussels Conventions* as given and sets forth the additional provisions or the options applicable in national legislation.

Geographical Scope

The limitations on the scope of the *Paris Convention* do not apply to the liability of an operator of an installation on Dutch territory, for damage: a) suffered on the territory of a State party to the Convention wherever the incident occurred; b) suffered on the territory of a State not party to the *Paris Convention*, but party to the *Joint Protocol* as the result of an incident in the territory of a State party to the *Joint Protocol*; or c) wherever suffered, as the result of an accident on Dutch territory.

Exonerations

Under the Dutch legislation, the operator is not exonerated from paying compensation for damage caused by an incident due directly to a grave natural disaster.

Carriage of Nuclear Materials

In relation to an incident on Dutch territory, the consignor and carrier of the nuclear substances involved in the incident and also the person holding the substances at that time shall be deemed to be the operator of a nuclear installation in Dutch territory and shall be held jointly and severally liable for the damage, unless it be proved that some other person is liable under either the *Paris Convention* or the *Joint Protocol*.

Amount of Liability

The maximum liability of the operator under the *Paris Convention* has been raised to Gld 625 million (approximately 240 million SDRs). Lower amounts have been established in relation to low risk installations.

Financial Security

If in the opinion of the Minister of Finance an operator of a nuclear installation cannot obtain the financial security required by the *Paris Convention* or if such financial security is only available at an unreasonable cost, the Minister may enter into contracts on behalf of the State as insurer or provide other State guarantees up to the operator's liability limit.

Time Limits

The time limit for personal injury claims is 30 years from the date of the accident; for other types of damage, the limit for submission of claims is ten years. In both cases, there is a limit of three years from the date the claimant had knowledge or ought reasonably to have had knowledge of both the damage and the operator liable.

Priorities

Claims filed within ten years of the date of the incident have priority over claims filed thereafter. However, in so far as the State provides supplementary funds beyond the *Brussels Convention* limit, at least ten percent of these funds will be reserved for personal injury claims filed after ten years. If there are both personal injury claims and other claims, two-thirds of each tier of compensation will be reserved for personal injury claims.

Competent Court and Procedures

If the damage caused by the nuclear incident is likely to exceed the operator's liability limit, claims must be brought before the District Court at The Hague, which has exclusive jurisdiction as the court of first instance. A prohibition will be placed on the payment of damages and a committee will be established to settle the claims under the authority of an examining judge. The committee is entitled to appoint and consult experts. If a claim is contested and the judge cannot reconcile the parties, he shall refer them to one or more court sessions for decision of the point at issue.

State Intervention

In so far as the funds becoming available from the operator's financial security are insufficient to compensate for the damage, the State shall make available funds up to his maximum liability. In such cases, the Minister is entitled to exercise the operator's right of recourse. If the damage caused by a nuclear incident in Netherlands territory exceeds the 300-million-SDR limit of the *Brussels Convention*, the Government will make available supplementary funds, to the effect that the total compensation available is Gld 5 billion guilders. These public funds will also be made available for damage suffered in the territory of parties to the *Brussels Convention* on condition of reciprocity.

Poland

General

At present, Poland has no functioning nuclear power plants. Although it had been committed to a nuclear power programme, after the accident at Chernobyl work on the plants under construction was suspended. In 1990 Poland became a party to the *Vienna Convention on Civil Liability for Nuclear Damage* and the *Joint Protocol*. However, as the law on nuclear liability – in the *Atomic Energy Act* – was adopted in 1986, it does not conform precisely to the current provisions of the Convention. Moreover, as Poland considers that its law provides superior protection, instead of changing the Act, the government has been active in submitting proposals to amend the Convention.

Nature of Liability

The operator of a nuclear installation is absolutely and exclusively liable for damage caused by the operation of the installation and by nuclear materials in the course of carriage under his responsibility.

Exonerations

The operator is exonerated from liability when damage is caused by acts of war or by the intentional fault of the victim.

Amount of Liability

In the Act, there is no limit on liability: the operator is liable for all the consequences of an incident causing nuclear damage.

Damage and Compensation

The most notable feature of the Polish legislation is that damage to the environment is covered, as well as damage caused to persons and property. The latter damage includes personal injury or damage to health, losses resulting from the destruction and deterioration of his property and lost earnings, as well as losses caused to the heirs by a death. Also covered are protective or preventive measures taken in response to an incident, in order to prevent persons and the environment from being exposed to ionising radiation. Persons injured during rescue operations are entitled to compensation.

Compensation for damage to the environment is claimed by the Treasury and the moneys paid into the Environmental Protection Fund.

Financial Security

Under the Act, the operator is required to take out insurance; however, the authorities have not yet determined the amount to be required.

Time Limits

There is no time limit to bringing claims for personal injury. The limit for damage to property and the environment is ten years from the date of the accident.

Competent Court

The ordinary rules of civil procedure apply, giving a choice between the court in the place of residence of the defendant or the place where the accident occurred.

State Intervention

When claims for personal injury exceed the amount of financial security, compensation may be claimed from the State as of right. The Council of Ministers is responsible for procedures to compensate damage to property and the environment exceeding the amount of insurance.

Switzerland

General

In 1993, Switzerland had five nuclear power plants with a capacity of 2,980 MWe. Although it has signed the *Paris* and *Brussels Conventions* and the *Joint Protocol*, Switzerland is not party to any of them. Nuclear liability is governed by the Act of 18 March 1983 on *Nuclear Third Party Liability*, as amended. While the Swiss law on liability resembles the legislation of parties to the *Paris Convention* in some respects, it also exhibits certain novel features, especially with regard to the amount of liability and the functioning of State intervention. As with other liability laws, the Swiss act applies to nuclear damage caused by accidents in nuclear installations and in the course of the carriage of nuclear materials.

Nature of Liability

In Switzerland, the liability of the operator is both absolute and exclusive. However, if the operator is not also the owner, the owner is jointly liable with the operator.

Exonerations

The operator is not liable to a victim who has caused the damage either intentionally or by gross negligence. He is not exonerated in the event of an accident due to armed conflict or a natural disaster.

Amount of Liability

The liability of the operator is unlimited. If the claims exceed the operator's financial security, compensation is paid in three layers: (1) by private insurance up to SF 500 million; (2) by the Confederation (the State) from SF 500 million up to SF 1 billion (495 million SDRs); and then, (3) by all the assets of the person liable.

Damage Covered

In the Act, nuclear damage is defined as damage caused by the hazardous properties of nuclear substances during the operation of a nuclear installation or in the course of carriage. In contrast to the conventions, Swiss law also includes as damage the cost of measures recommended by the authorities to avert or to mitigate an immediately threatening nuclear danger. Deferred damage, appearing after the 30 year limitation period is compensated by the State.

Financial Security

All operators must maintain insurance for SF 500 million for each nuclear installation, plus at least SF 50 million for legal expenses and interest. In the case of the transit of nuclear materials through Switzerland, insurance cover must be at least SF 50 million, plus SF 5 million for interest and expenses. Under the terms of the Act, the amount of financial security is raised from time to time, when the insurance market offers higher cover. The Confederation is not required to take out insurance for the installations that it operates itself. In accordance with an ordinance of the Federal Council, insurers are entitled to exclude certain risks from coverage. Compensation for these risks is then provided by the Confederation (see State Intervention).

Time Limits

There is a three year discovery rule and a limit of 30 years from the date of the accident, except in the case of deferred damage.

Competent Court

Each canton is to designate a single court to hear claims for nuclear damage caused by an accident taking place within that canton.

Compensation

After a serious nuclear accident, the Federal Council will order an inquiry to identify the injured parties. A published notice will request them to make themselves known and to provide basic information about the damage. Victims may proceed directly against the insurers and the Confederation within the amount covered by the insurance. The nature and extent of compensation is governed by the ordinary civil law. However, if the victim has an unusually high income, the court may reduce the compensation on equitable terms. If the proceedings are likely to last some time, the court may award provisional payments. Where the Confederation provides compensation for special cases, it may reduce or refuse payment if the victim has caused the damage through gross negligence.

State Intervention

The Confederation plays a role in compensating the victims of nuclear damage in the following three cases.

The Nuclear Damage Fund – Managed by the Federal Energy Office, the Fund operates as secondary insurance to cover nuclear operators for compensation amounts beyond those provided by private insurance, up to the SF 1 billion limit, and for excluded risks, which include deferred damage manifested after the 30-year limit, accidents caused by armed conflict and natural disasters, and claims made more than 20 years after loss, theft, abandonment or cessation of possession of nuclear substances. The Fund is financed by annual premiums paid by nuclear operators.

Special Cases – In the following special cases, the Confederation will pay compensation out of its own resources:

a) where the person liable cannot be identified;

b) where the damage is caused by an uninsured nuclear installation or an uninsured transport operation;

c) where the insurer and the person liable are insolvent;

d) where a person who has suffered nuclear damage in Switzerland as a result of an accident abroad cannot obtain in the country concerned compensation equivalent to that available under the Act.

Compensation for damage caused by Chernobyl was provided under the latter provision.

Major Occurrences If there is reason to believe that the insurance cover will not satisfy all the claims, the Confederation will establish a special indemnity scheme to determine principles for the equitable distribution of funds, make special provisions regarding rights of recourse and insurance, etc. In addition, the Confederation may compensate the damage not otherwise covered.

United Kingdom

General

In the United Kingdom, there are 35 power reactors with a net electrical capacity of 11,900 MWe, and one under construction. The United Kingdom is a party to both the *Paris* and the *Brussels Conventions* and has signed but not ratified the *Joint Protocol*. The basic legislation on liability for nuclear damage is contained in the *Nuclear Installations Act* of 1965, as amended. Generally, the Act implements the provisions of the *Paris* and *Vienna Conventions*. Under the Act the licensee (operator) of a nuclear installation has a duty to secure that no occurrence or incident involving nuclear material or the emission of ionising radiation (on-site) for which he is responsible causes personal injury or damage to property other than his own. The operator is absolutely and exclusively liable for a breach of that duty.

Exonerations

The operator is exonerated only if a nuclear accident or the damage that it occasions is attributable to hostile action in the course of armed conflict.

Amount of Liability

The liability of a British nuclear operator is limited to £140 million, (approximately 150 million SDRs) except in the case of lesser risks, for which the limit is £5 million.

Damage and Compensation

Generally, the damage covered is the same as in the *Paris Convention*. However, if a child is born disabled as a result of exposure of a parent to ionizing radiation caused by a nuclear accident, the operator will be liable as if the child had been injured at the same time as the parent.

Limits

Actions for damage must be brought within 30 years of the date of the accident.

Competent Court

Although all British high courts have concurrent jurisdiction, the Secretary of State may certify that claims must be brought before a certain court. Likewise, the Secretary of State may certify that a foreign court has jurisdiction over a particular case.

State Intervention

Under the British legislation, all claims are to be met in full if possible, up to the limit of 300 million SDRs of the *Brussels Convention* in the case of victims in the States party to that Convention. The State will pay compensation for claims made more than ten years after the accident.

United States

General

In the United States, there are 109 nuclear power plants with a total output of 98,700 MWe, and two more under instruction. The United States is not a party to any of the conventions on civil liability, and its law on nuclear liability is rather different from the systems of the *Paris* and *Vienna Conventions*. The only nuclear installations close enough to affect American territory (and vice versa) in the event of an accident are those of Canada. To address the question of compensation for nuclear damage, the two countries have concluded a bilateral arrangement providing for mutual benefits.

The American law on liability for nuclear damage is contained in the *Price-Anderson Act*, which forms part of the *Atomic Energy* Act of 1954. Originally enacted in 1957, the *Price-Anderson Act* has been revised several times since, most recently in 1988. The current law will expire in the year 2002. One of the most unusual features of this federal law is that it does not treat the substantive issues regarding liability for damage. Instead, the applicable law is that of the State where the reactor is located, with the result that in some States there would be strict liability and in others, liability for fault. Second, legal liability is not channelled to the operator. However, financial security is required and liability is limited.

In the United States, private nuclear facilities (such as power plants) and materials are licensed and regulated by the Nuclear Regulatory Commission (NRC), while government-owned facilities are within the jurisdiction of the Department of Energy (DOE).

Extraordinary Nuclear Occurrences

Notwithstanding the general rules which apply in the case of "ordinary" accidents, special provisions prevail in the case of an "extraordinary nuclear occurrence" (ENO). An ENO is defined as being any event causing a discharge of nuclear material which the NRC or the Secretary of Energy determines to be substantial, and which the NRC or the Secretary of Energy determines has resulted or will probably result in substantial damages to persons or property "off site".

Scope

The *Price-Anderson Act* applies to nuclear accidents occurring within the United States and causing damage either within or outside U.S. territory, as well as to precautionary evacuations, when there is a situation of imminent danger, but no accident, as defined, has actually occurred. Furthermore, the Act applies to accidents occurring outside the United States involving nuclear material owned by, used by, or under contract with the United States or nuclear material licensed by the Nuclear Regulatory Commission (NRC). The Act covers both NRC-licensed and DOE activities, including the DOE's activities relating to radioactive waste.

Basis of Liability

As the *Price-Anderson Act* does not contain any provisions on the basis of liability for nuclear damage, the matter falls to be settled in accordance with State law. As each State has its own law concerning liability for damage, the principles to be applied will vary between strict liability and liability for fault according to

81

the law in the State where the accident occurred. In the case of an ENO, all defences under State law will be waived, with the result that any liability will effectively be absolute. The NRC and the DOE are authorised to include such waivers in any indemnity agreements or to require their incorporation in any approved financial security.

Lack of Exclusive Liability

As already noted, legal liability is not channelled to the operator. Consequently, contractors, suppliers, carriers, etc., may be sued for damage. However, U.S. law does provide for economic channelling, in that the financial security held by the operator covers all the other persons who may be held liable. In most cases, it is the operator who would be sued; nevertheless, even if another party is judged liable, the financial security of the operator will provide funds for compensation. In the case of DOE contractors, the government provides a full indemnity, up to the same liability limit as the highest one for private operators.

Exonerations

Under the *Price-Anderson Act*, exonerations are permitted in the case of claims for workmen's compensation, claims arising from an act of war, claims by persons having intentionally caused the accident or the damage, in addition to exonerations under State law.

Amount of Liability

Under the Act, liability is limited to approximately $8.96 billion (6.3 billion SDRs), including administrative and legal expenses. In the case of power plants licensed by the NRC, this amount is comprised of a primary layer of $200 million per reactor from individual financial security, such as insurance, plus a second layer consisting of an industry pool funded by a retrospective premium of $75.5 million contributed by each reactor in the United States. To alleviate the burden on the operators, no more than $10 million may be paid in any one year and the total may be spread over seven or more years. Every five years, the amount of the premium is to be adjusted in accordance with the change in the consumer price index. For contractors indemnified by the DOE, the liability limit is the same. Compensation for accidents involving radioactive waste will be paid by DOE from the Nuclear Waste Fund.

In the case of other NRC licensees required to maintain financial protection, the limit of liability is: (a) the financial security of the licensee, plus a

$500 million government indemnity; or (b) if the security exceeds $60 million, $560 million or the amount of financial security, whichever is greater. For DOE indemnifications involving accidents outside the United States, the limit is $100 million. For non-profit educational institutions (e.g., for university research reactors), the limit is $250,000, plus a $500 million NRC indemnity.

Financial Security

Each licence to construct or operate a nuclear installation must, and each licence to possess and use nuclear material may require that the licensee maintain authorised financial security. The amount required is the amount available at reasonable cost and terms from private sources. For large power reactors, this is currently $200 million. Furthermore, the operators of large power reactors must maintain private insurance to provide funds for retrospective premiums of up to $75.5 million per reactor, if the primary cover of $200 million is insufficient to compensate all the damage. In special cases, smaller amounts may be authorised. At present, both the primary cover and funds for the industry pool are provided by the two American nuclear insurance pools. Finally, an NRC regulation requires operators to maintain a minimum amount of material damage insurance, the proceeds of which must be applied first to stabilise a damaged reactor and to remove contamination from the installation to the extent that it poses a threat to the public.

Neither federal agencies nor non-profit educational institutions are required to maintain financial security, but the NRC must enter into indemnification agreements with such agencies or institutions, except for the DOE.

Damage Covered

As well as death or personal injury and loss of or damage to property, the Act covers damage caused by a precautionary evacuation of the public within an area specified by the State or local government official authorised to order a precautionary evacuation. As a response to the failure of local governments to recover their response costs in litigation relating to the accident at Three Mile Island, under the 1988 amendments to the Act, federal government indemnities will include compensation to local governments for their response costs. However, operators are still not liable for these costs under their insurance policies. Similarly, operators' insurance does not cover liability for damage to the environment; however, as government indemnity includes "any legal liability arising out of or resulting from a nuclear incident", damage to the environment might be included. Immediate assistance is provided by the insurers to persons required to leave their homes as the result of a nuclear accident.

Unlike the provisions of the international conventions, the *Price-Anderson Act* stipulates that administration costs and legal expenses are included within the liability limit, but subject to judicial control.

Time Limits

Although the *Price-Anderson Act* does not lay down any final time limit, in the event of an ENO, the waiver of defences is effective only where an action is brought within three years of discovery.

Competent Court and Procedure

The 1988 amendments to the *Price-Anderson Act* provide that the competent court is the United States District court in the district where the accident occurred, except in the case of an accident outside the United States, when the competent court is the United States District Court for the District of Columbia, whatever the citizenship of the plaintiff.

State Intervention

If it appears that the necessary amount of retrospective premiums will not be available on time through the resources of private industry and insurance, the NRC may provide reinsurance or may guarantee the payment of such premiums. Furthermore, if the funds available to pay claims in any year are inadequate because of the $10 million per reactor limit, the NRC may advance the necessary funds, by means of a request to Congress or a loan from the U.S. Treasury. Reimbursement will be obtained from the operators in due course.

Also, the NRC will indemnify non-profit educational institutions for liability between $250,000 and $500 million, and federal agencies other than DOE for up to $500 million. Finally, as noted above, the DOE will indemnify its contractors up to an $8.96 billion limit. However, this indemnity for government contractors does not mean that they do not have to "pay" if they cause an accident, for they are liable to fines and penalties for breaches of the regulations.

The 1988 amendments incorporate the basic principle of full compensation. If the claims are likely to exceed $8.96 billion, the U.S. Congress will review the situation and will take the action necessary to provide full and prompt compensation of the damage. In order to assist the Congress, the President is required to submit a comprehensive compensation plan within 90 days of a court determination that liability for any nuclear accident may exceed the liability limit. In response, Congress may appropriate the funds necessary to provide full compensation.

The Presidential Commission on Catastrophic Accidents

Under the 1988 amendments to the *Price-Anderson Act*, a Presidential Commission was appointed to study the means of fully compensating victims of a catastrophic nuclear accident, where the amount of damage exceeds the liability limit. In August 1990, the Commission produced a report proposing a system of equitable compensation, with recommendations on civil procedures, claim priorities, and standards and procedures for dealing with latent injuries.

In its report, the Commission expressed the belief that applying the common law principles of actions for damages would result in either an outright denial of recovery or a difficult and protracted process. Instead of approaching the problem from the perspective of liability, the Commission envisioned the Price-Anderson system as a vast insurance programme, protecting potential claimants against a large accident at a nuclear installation. The following are summaries of the four specific recommendations:

1.   The appropriate "trigger" for the application of its recommendations should be a finding by the court that there is a reasonable likelihood of claims exceeding the basic level of insurance ($200 million), so that recourse to retrospective premiums would be necessary. At this point, the financing effects would have national ramifications.

2.   The Commission recommended that claims be settled through a judicial process containing administrative features designed to speed the resolution of cases. The distribution scheme, including emergency and final payments, would be co-ordinated by the competent Court. To consider generic issues and provide advice, the court would appoint a Panel of Scientific Advisors. The court would then decide generic issues, such as a schedule of compensation for non-pecuniary injuries, the determination of proximate cause, and the resolution of factual disputes that are medical or scientific in character. Examples of the latter would be determination of the level of exposure sufficient to justify provision for medical monitoring and the level of contamination that would necessitate permanent abandonment of property and hence compensation for loss.

Settlement of claims would be encouraged, recourse to one of two dispute resolution options should be required, and arbitration should be available to all claimants before final recourse to plenary adjudication.

3. Compensation for losses occasioned by a nuclear accident or a precautionary evacuation would be provided on the following basis:

   a) claims for pecuniary losses would be compensated in full;

   b) claims for latent illnesses, death and pain and suffering would be paid on a scheduled basis; future illness would be compensated through a medical monitoring system; and emotional distress would be compensated through counselling;

   c) punitive damages would be prohibited.

4. The Commission recommended that pecuniary and non-pecuniary claims arising from latent health effects be compensated on the basis of probability of causation methodology. Because it is impossible to prove that any particular illness, such as cancer, was caused by any particular nuclear accident, a causal relation would have to be based upon an association between the radiation exposure and a particular illness. Those who exhibit a strong association – it is more likely than not that the illness occurred as a result of the accident – would receive full compensation. On the other hand, where it is extremely unlikely that the illness resulted from the accident, no payment would be made. For probabilities between the two limits, there would be some proportional recovery related to the likelihood of causation.

Chapter VI

THE ACCIDENT AT CHERNOBYL AND THE NEED FOR CHANGE

The Accident at Chernobyl

On 26 April 1986, there was a severe nuclear accident in Unit 4 of the nuclear power plant at Chernobyl, in the former Soviet Union. Radioactive gas escaping after a chemical explosion and the resulting fire formed into a large cloud that dispersed rapidly over most of Europe, eventually reaching North America and even Japan. During the first two days, the radioactive cloud moved in a northwesterly direction, towards Finland and Sweden. Then it turned to the southeast, traversing Poland, Czechoslovakia and southern Germany, before returning northwards to the Netherlands. In the course of the next few days, the radioactive particles moved south into Austria and northern Italy, and westwards across France to reach the United Kingdom on the second of May.

The occurrence of the accident was first detected when Swedish monitoring equipment registered abnormally high levels of radioactivity. Subsequently, radioactivity in the air was monitored by all affected countries, with 15 radionuclides being identified with certainty. Both the amount of radioactivity and the type of radionuclides varied considerably from place to place depending upon the air currents, the terrain, and most importantly, precipitation. The passage of the radioactive cloud was marked by the deposition of dry particles on the ground, with the high ground becoming the most contaminated.

Unfortunately, rainshowers in certain regions, as the cloud was moving to the north and west, provoked the deposition of certain nuclides from 10 to 100 times the rate of deposition of dry particles. Naturally, the absolute level of the contamination by radioactive rain depended upon the intensity of the precipitation and the distribution of the various substances in the cloud. The situation was complicated by the fact that the cloud passed back and forth over Europe during a period of several days, thereby exposing the public to radioactivity during a longer period than would have been the case in the event of a single passage.

Emergency Response and Damage Close to the Accident

Once the Soviet authorities recognised the seriousness of the accident, they called in the army to put out the fire and stabilise the situation in the reactor. At the same time, the inhabitants of a 30-kilometre "exclusion zone" surrounding the power plant were evacuated and resettled elsewhere, as were the population of an "outer zone" also affected by radioactive contamination. The area surrounding the reactor is still so contaminated that no one may live there permanently. Even further off, produce from farms where there is a high level of radioactivity cannot be sold. Although the official death toll from the accident is 31, all of them working on the emergency response, a much greater number of victims is to be feared. However, although it is known that the emergency workers and some of the evacuees suffer from health problems, no official study has yet been published on their situation.

On the other hand, Russian experts have published information on the compensation paid to victims by the Soviet and later, Russian, State. By 1990, over 200 billion roubles had been paid for direct and indirect material losses, and 2.5 billion on compensation and concessions to victims. In 1991-92, this expenditure was financed under the long-term State programme of emergency measures to deal with the consequences of the accident at the Chernobyl power plant. In other words, civil liability was not involved; compensation is being paid under administrative procedures.

Compensation is being paid to invalids for damage to health and to families for the loss of a breadwinner, with special arrangements for those who dealt with the consequences of the accident. The State assumes the cost of medical care. Those who were evacuated were paid for the loss of their homes and property, crops, livestock, etc., and were given a lump-sum grant. Costs to the State included those of resettlement and the loss of economic activity. In addition to compensation, some victims have also been accorded various socio-economic, housing pension, tax and other concessions.

The type and amount of the concessions depends upon the category of the victim: citizens who have contracted or had radiation sickness or other diseases associated with the radiation dose; persons who have acquired disability causally connected with the accident; citizens who participated in dealing with its consequences; those employed in running the Chernobyl nuclear power plant; those evacuated from the exclusion zone of the plant; as well as other categories of persons who previously lived or worked, or are currently living or working in the contaminated territories.

As soon as the authorities in the affected States became aware of what they considered to be dangerous levels of radioactivity in the air, water and soil, they took immediate measures in order to protect public health. Because of the high levels of radioactivity in precipitation, the first interventions consisted of recommendations not to drink rainwater. These interventions were based upon the dose levels recommended by the International Commission on Radiological Protection (ICRP). In some places the recommended maximum limit would have been exceeded in one day if the rainwater had been drunk.

The International Commission on Radiological Protection

The ICRP is a private association of international experts elected on purely scientific grounds, who are independent of any political or commercial interest. The mission of the ICRP is to provide advice on radiation protection, including specific recommendations and guidelines on the degrees of exposure to ionising radiation that will have deleterious effects. The purpose is to assist regulatory and advisory agencies, as well as managements of nuclear installations and their professional staff, to formulate and implement regulations and procedures to protect human beings from the detrimental effects of ionising radiation. The recommendations of the ICRP are issued in a series of publications that are periodically revised and updated. The latest revision was published in 1991 as ICRP Publication No. 60.

Both the rain and the dry deposition of radionuclides rapidly contaminated grass and other vegetation, with the result that cows that had been put out to pasture gave milk containing abnormally high levels of radioactivity. While in the north, most cattle were still being kept indoors, in the south they were already out to pasture. In Italy, the level of iodine 131 reached 2,000 becquerels per litre, while in the U.K. values of 50 becquerels per litre were identified in the south and 400 per litre in the north, where the rainfall was greater. On 26 May 1986, the European Community adopted an intervention level for milk of 125 becquerels per litre. (A becquerel (Bq) is the unit of measurement for the activity of radioactive substances. See Chapter VII for an explanation of intervention levels.)

In some countries, it was recommended that animals be fed in their stables, while in all countries, the sale of milk was restricted or banned. High levels of radioactivity were also found in seasonal vegetables, such as lettuce and spinach, with the sale of such produce being prohibited in some countries.

In western Europe, the damage caused by Chernobyl consisted mainly in damage to the environment – air, soil, water, fauna and flora – to agriculture, and a lesser extent to non-farming property contaminated by airborne radioactivity. Throughout Europe, east and west, farmers, fishermen, those herding livestock, mushroom and berry pickers and others suffered heavy losses when the sale of their produce was restricted either at home or abroad. In most countries, compensation was provided by each State to the victims within their own jurisdiction. For example, in the Federal Republic of Germany, DM 500 million marks were paid out under the liability provisions of the *Atomic Energy Law* and associated administrative procedures.

The duration of radioactivity has the effect of extending the damage, either for decades, or, closest to the accident, for centuries. For example, the soil upon which radionuclides have been deposited may remain contaminated for many years, thus precluding the growing of crops or the raising of livestock. In the United Kingdom, it has been estimated that some land contaminated by fallout from Chernobyl may remain unusable for grazing sheep for 30 years. Care will also have to be taken in relation to foods canned or frozen soon after the accident that may be consumed months or years later, as well as to beasts that may be slaughtered years after the nuclear accident.

Another kind of damage involves food moving in international trade. After a nuclear accident, the authorities in third countries may ban the import of food and other products coming from areas close to the site of the accident, either entirely, or if it is contaminated above a certain level. This was done by the European Union in relation to food and feedstuffs bearing prescribed levels of radioactivity caused by the accident at Chernobyl. These import bans have only recently begun to be phased out.

The problem of contaminated food may affect trade even further afield. For example, in late January 1988, 17 pounds of French mushrooms were quarantined at Tokyo Airport, after officials detected 636 Bq of radioactivity per kilogram in the mushrooms, when the danger level was set at 370 Bq by the Japanese health and welfare ministry. A similar problem would occur even if the food were not banned, but people were afraid of buying it.

International Co-operation in Response

The accident at Chernobyl revealed substantial inadequacies in relation to nuclear safety, emergency response and liability to compensate for nuclear damage. In response, individual countries and the responsible international organisations reviewed and revised their programmes dealing with nuclear emergencies. At the international level, the main organisations are the IAEA, the OECD/NEA and the European Union,. Since Chernobyl, all three have placed an increased emphasis on safety and emergency response, with the IAEA and the NEA also making a concerted effort to improve the international regime of liability for nuclear damage.

Nuclear Safety

In relation to safety, both the NEA and the IAEA have enhanced and adjusted their programmes, with the IAEA in particular greatly expanding its safety services in response to increased demand from member States. Most recently, in 1994, the members of the IAEA adopted a new *Nuclear Safety Convention* to make what are already existing practices in most States with nuclear power plants binding under international law, and to extend the legal obligations to States where these safety practices have not yet been adopted. Although the general subject of nuclear safety is beyond the scope of this study, as noted in Chapter IX, the *Safety Convention* may be relevant to a revised liability regime.

Emergency Response

In relation to emergency response, which had been relatively neglected, both the NEA and the IAEA rapidly developed new programmes to address the failings that had been exposed. The NEA focused its attention on the determination of the most appropriate measures to be taken in an emergency situation. Among the issues faced by the IAEA was that of the notification of an accident and assistance to the States most affected. When the accident occurred, the USSR government kept silent for two entire days, telling no one, neither the local population, nor the international community. Under international law, this was a violation of the duty under customary law to warn other States of impending danger. Furthermore, the failure to warn was also inconsistent with the political and moral commitment in certain non-binding guidelines adopted by the IAEA in 1984.

In the event, those who suffered most were the Soviet people themselves, especially those living in areas of Belarus, Ukraine and Russia closest to the reactor or within the path of the cloud of radioactive substances emitted from it. An early warning, coupled with information on how to protect themselves, could have helped many of the inhabitants to avoid the worst of the potential harm. Of course, if the power plant had been situated near a border, it would have been the inhabitants of another country who were in danger of being exposed to levels of ionising radiation high enough to cause serious damage to human health. With a proper emergency plan and a quick response by the national authorities, those within the danger zone could have been evacuated, advised to take shelter, administered prophylactic doses of iodine, and so forth.

As a result of the delayed and disorderly response to Chernobyl, States realised that they had to institute an early warning system to enable themselves to react as quickly as possible to prevent or mitigate the damage whenever and wherever an accident occurred. For ideological reasons, the former USSR found it difficult to accept the existence of an international obligation under general legal principles or customary international law. That is, it only recognised as binding upon it international treaties to which it had given its consent. As a consequence, the IAEA member States decided immediately to conclude two international conventions on the subjects of the early notification of a nuclear accident and international co-operation to assist affected States.

The Conventions on Notification *and* Assistance

Due to the sense of urgency created by the Chernobyl disaster, to the existence of models in the agreed IAEA guidelines, and to the awareness of the participants that international co-operation was vital to improving emergency response before the next accident, the texts of the two conventions were prepared and adopted in record time. The same sense of urgency also induced an unusually rapid accumulation of ratifications, so that the *Convention on Early Notification of a Nuclear Accident* came into force on 27 October 1986 and the *Convention on Assistance in the Case of a Nuclear Accident or Radiological Emergency* on 26 February 1987.

The primary obligation of States parties to the *Convention on Early Notification* is to notify, either directly or through the IAEA, all the States which are or may be affected, of a nuclear accident, its nature, the time of its occurrence and its exact location. Thus duly notified, the affected States will be able to take the appropriate measures in response. The purpose of the *Convention on Assistance* is to establish an international framework to facilitate the prompt

92

provision of assistance to mitigate the consequences of a nuclear accident or radiological emergency. Under the Convention, the parties agree to co-operate among themselves and with the IAEA to protect life, property and the environment from radiological releases.

Importance of Emergency Response in Relation to Liability

Of course, the primary importance of effective emergency response is to prevent or to mitigate any potential injury or damage arising from an accident. However, an appropriate response is also significant in relation to liability for damage. There are two reasons for this. First, a rapid and effective emergency response should reduce the amount of damage that remains to be compensated. Secondly, and as a logical consequence, the cost of such preventive or protective measures taken in response to an accident could be made compensable under the conventions, in order to provide an incentive for potential victims to mitigate their damage and to cover their expenses of doing so.

In fact, compensation for preventive measures is already available under the maritime conventions relating to liability for oil pollution damage. Using the oil pollution conventions as a model, some States believe that the *Vienna Convention* should be revised to provide for such compensation in relation to nuclear accidents. In the view of those States proposing the change, payment for such measures is justified by the fact that it is preferable and less expensive to prevent or to minimise the severity of the damage in the first instance, rather than to pay for it afterwards, especially as some of the damage may be irreparable.

The *Joint Protocol Relating to the Application of the Paris Convention and the Vienna Convention*

The inadequacy of the existing regime for international liability became apparent when the Soviet Union refused to accept responsibility for the damage in other States caused by the radioactive fallout from the accident at Chernobyl. As already noted, the USSR maintained that it was not responsible for transboundary harm unless it was a party to an internationally binding agreement in which it had expressly accepted such liability. The USSR was not a party to the *Vienna Convention on Civil Liability* and there is no convention on State liability for damage arising from nuclear accidents. In the earlier case of the Cosmos 954 nuclear powered satellite that fell to earth in the Canadian north in January 1978, the USSR agreed to pay to Canada 3 million dollars in damages precisely because both countries were parties to the *Convention on International Liability for Damage Caused by Space Objects.*

The Problem of Insufficient Geographical Coverage

Looking to the future, it was clear that before another accident occurred, some means had to be found to induce the USSR and other non-parties to adhere to an international agreement providing compensation for damage arising from a nuclear accident. Although the *Vienna Convention* was theoretically open to universal adherence, very few States had become parties, mainly because they considered it to be seriously deficient and contrary to the "polluter-pays" principle. Therefore, after the accident at Chernobyl, many States wished immediately to begin negotiations for the revision of the *Vienna Convention.* These States believed that if the deficiencies of the civil liability regime were remedied by a careful and comprehensive reworking of the *Vienna Convention*, more States, including the Soviet Union, could be induced to become parties.

However, other States believed that the civil liability system was insufficient and would not provide adequate protection for the public. They insisted that only a new convention on direct State liability could provide adequate protection – first, because States are responsible for ensuring the safety of and for preventing accidents in nuclear facilities under their jurisdiction or control, and second, because only States possess the resources to provide prompt, adequate and effective compensation to the victims.

Yet, even if it were decided to revise the *Vienna Convention*, and if the Convention were much improved, that would not resolve the problem of adequate geographical coverage where it was most imperative – on the European continent. For it was in Europe that the greatest number of nuclear reactors were situated (over 200 of a total of about 400), as well as some of the most dangerous, and it was in Europe that transboundary liability issues were most likely to arise, due to the large number of countries within a relatively small geographic area.

At the time of Chernobyl, 14 OECD Member countries of western Europe were party to the *Paris Convention*, while no countries in eastern Europe, except Yugoslavia were party to the *Vienna Convention.* Furthermore, since they had their own instrument, the parties to the *Paris Convention* had no interest in becoming parties to the *Vienna Convention* either. Thus, the *Paris* and *Vienna Conventions* existed in complete isolation from each other. As a consequence, victims in a party to one convention could not claim compensation under either

94

convention for damage arising from an accident in a State party to the other convention. Therefore, even if the USSR and other Eastern European countries became parties to the *Vienna Convention*, the problem for potential west European claimants would not be resolved.

In fact, the problem of the lack of a relationship between the two civil liability conventions had been recognised some years earlier. In the mid-1970s, discussions had begun on the creation of a link between the *Paris* and *Vienna Conventions*. Although a few drafts for a *Joint Protocol* had been prepared, the negotiations had been suspended for lack of sufficient political interest. In September 1986, after some inconclusive debate regarding the issue of State liability and the revision of the *Vienna Convention* at the IAEA General Conference, the same sense of urgency that had led to the adoption of the *Conventions on Notification* and *Assistance*, impelled the liability issue to an interim solution.

During the debate on liability at the 1986 General Conference, it was therefore considered that the time was ripe for a combined meeting of the IAEA and NEA secretariats to consider a proposal to resume work on a joint protocol. Many States believed that the existence of a link to the *Paris Convention*, coupled with a revision of the *Vienna Convention* would induce the Central and Eastern European States to join the *Vienna Convention*, thereby extending the benefits of the international civil liability regime throughout the continent. Within a few months the IAEA and the NEA had established a joint Group of Governmental Experts to engage in negotiations that culminated in the adoption, at a diplomatic conference in September 1988, of the *Joint Protocol Relating to the Application of the Paris Convention and the Vienna Convention.*

Functioning of the Joint Protocol

The *Joint Protocol* deals with the civil liability of the operators of nuclear installations governed by both the *Paris* and the *Vienna Conventions*. Hence, it applies to nuclear damage caused by accidents occurring in land-based nuclear installations and during the transport of nuclear materials thereto and therefrom. The *Joint Protocol* fulfills two functions. First, by abolishing the status of non-contracting State as between the parties to the *Paris* and *Vienna Conventions*, it permits victims in States party to either of the Conventions to obtain compensation for an accident occurring in a State party to the other. Thus, if Ukraine became a party to both the *Vienna Convention* and the *Joint Protocol* and if there were another accident at Chernobyl, then victims in the *Paris Convention*

States which were also parties to the *Joint Protocol* could sue for damages the operator of the Chernobyl nuclear power plant.

Secondly, in addition to creating this system of mutual benefits, the *Joint Protocol* also prevents conflicts of jurisdiction by ensuring that only one convention is applied to any one nuclear accident.

Article I defines the two conventions as including any amendment that is in force for the party to the *Joint Protocol*. This was to ensure that the *1982 Protocol* amending the *Paris Convention* would be included when it came into force. Similarly, any future amendment to the *Vienna Convention* will also be applicable when it comes into force.

Article II abolishes the distinction between contracting and non-contracting parties as regards the *Paris* and *Vienna Conventions* by extending the respective operator liability to nuclear damage suffered in the territories of the parties to the other convention. The liability of the operator is determined in accordance with the provisions of the convention to which he is subject, that is, the convention to which the installation State is a party. Thus, his limitation of liability will be that established in his national legislation. Although neither the *Paris* nor the *Vienna Convention* refers to nuclear incidents occurring or to nuclear damage suffered on or above the high seas, there is general agreement that both conventions apply to such cases.

Article III implements the second function of the *Joint Protocol*, by providing that either the *Paris* or the *Vienna Convention* shall apply to the exclusion of the other. In the case of incidents occurring in nuclear installations, the convention adhered to by the State in which the installation is situated will apply. In the case of the transportation of nuclear materials, the relevant provisions of the two Conventions (which are virtually identical), shall determine which convention is applicable.

Article IV simply specifies that all the operative articles of each convention are to be applied, but that the merely procedural articles shall be excluded. The operative articles are those dealing with liability amounts, financial cover, recourse and subrogation, jurisdiction and enforcement of judgements, as well as with compensation and its equitable distribution. It is interesting to note that even those articles in the *Paris Convention* that have no counterpart in the *Vienna Convention* are to be applied.

Other Issues

Not dealt with in the *Joint Protocol* are the issues of the differences between the *Paris* and *Vienna Conventions*, the need to revise them both, and the effect of the *Joint Protocol* upon the *Brussels Supplementary Convention.*

The *Joint Protocol* will affect the *Brussels Supplementary Convention* in two ways. First, because the geographical scope of the *Paris Convention* will be extended to States which are not parties by including those in States party to the *Vienna Convention*, the funds available for compensation by the operator will be distributed among a larger number of victims. Consequently, the operator's financial limit will be reached more quickly, and an early call may be made upon State contributions to ensure full compensation to victims in *Paris Convention* States. Under the terms of the *Brussels Convention*, in this situation, express consent by all the parties will be required for the use of public funds in accidents to which the *Joint Protocol* applies.

Secondly, the application of the *Joint Protocol* will exclude the application of the *Brussels Convention* in certain transportation cases in which it would otherwise have come into play. This is because at some point liability will be transferred to an operator in a *Vienna Convention* State, instead of being retained by an operator subject to the *Paris Convention*. Consequently, victims in *Paris Convention* States will be denied the possibility of the higher level of compensation afforded by the State funds under the Brussels supplementary system.

In order to preserve the application of the *Brussels Convention* in these circumstances, the States parties have agreed to issue declarations consenting to the use of public funds in cases where the *Joint Protocol* applies, and to ensure under national law that a *Paris Convention* operator remains liable in transport cases involving *Vienna Convention* States.

Status of the Joint Protocol

The *Joint Protocol* came into force on 27 April 1992. At 1 October 1994, the parties were: Cameroon, Chile, Egypt, Hungary, Poland, Romania (*Vienna Convention*), Denmark, Italy, Norway, the Netherlands, and Sweden (*Paris Convention*). Since the adoption of the *Joint Protocol*, several additional States have acceded or succeeded to the *Vienna Convention*; Hungary, Poland, Chile, Mexico, Slovenia, Croatia, Lithuania, and Romania. Consequently, the coverage of the civil liability régime has increased substantially, especially in Europe.

Parties to the *Joint Protocol*

Signatories	Date of Ratification or Accession
Argentina (VC)	—
Belgium (PC)	—
Bulgaria (VC) (acc.)	24 August 1994
Cameroon (VC)	28 October 1991
Chile (VC)	23 November 1989
Croatia (VC)	10 May 1994
Czech Republic (VC) (acc.)	24 March 1994
Denmark (PC)	26 May 1989
Egypt (VC)	10 August 1989
Estonia (VC) (acc.)	9 May 1994
Finland (PC)	3 October 1994
France (PC)	—
Germany (PC)	—
Greece (PC)	—
Hungary (VC)	26 March 1990
Italy (PC)	31 July 1991
Lithuania (VC) (acc.)	20 September 1993
Morocco (VC)*	—
Netherlands (PC)	1 August 1991
Norway (PC)	11 March 1991
Philippines (VC)	—
Poland (VC) (acc.)	23 January 1990
Portugal (PC)	—
Romania (VC) (acc.)	29 December 1992
Spain (PC)	—
Sweden (PC)	27 January 1992
Switzerland (PC)*	—
Turkey (PC)	—
United Kingdom (PC)	—
Entry into force	*27 April 1992*

(PC) Paris Convention; (VC) Vienna Convention; * Signatory only of the Convention.

International State Liability

As noted above, after the accident at Chernobyl, while some States believed that the deficiencies of the civil liability system could be overcome by the adoption of the *Joint Protocol* and the revision of the *Vienna Convention*, other

States believed that the question of liability for nuclear damage could only be effectively addressed by the conclusion of a new convention on State liability. Initially, a fair number of States supported this option, in the context of both the IAEA and the Legal Committee of the United Nations. However, others opposed the idea, arguing that the law in the area was not sufficiently developed, or that it would be premature to begin work on a new convention before the International Law Commission (ILC) concluded its work on the general question of State liability.

Private International Law and Public International Law

Civil liability refers to the liability of a private party, either an individual human being or a "legal person", such as a company that is the operator of a nuclear power plant, to another individual or legal person, under private law in a domestic (national) legal system. Although they generally function under public law, if they choose, governments may be held liable or may sue under national or international private law. In the existing nuclear liability conventions, the liability exists exclusively under national or international *private law*, and any claims for damage are to be submitted to an ordinary court functioning in the national legal system of the country having jurisdiction over the accident. The claims are made under *private international law* if the plaintiff and the defendant are situated in different countries.

In contrast, the system of *public international law* (usually referred to simply as "international law"), regulates the legal relations between *States*. Where there exists a legal dispute between two States, the parties generally attempt to resolve it by means of diplomatic negotiations, or mediation (and occasionally conciliation), but if they choose, they may have recourse to arbitration or judicial settlement. In an *ad hoc* arbitration, the States involved choose the judges and the rules under which they operate; in judicial settlement, they bring the case before an already existing international court, such as the International Court of Justice or a special court established to deal with certain types of issues.

Because there is no international legislative body, the sources of international law are rather different from the sources of law in domestic legal systems. In general, these sources are international agreements (conventions), custom (State practice accepted as legally binding), general principles of law, and certain acts of international organisations (e.g., Decisions of the OECD Council). There is some doctrinal dispute as to the origins and the application of general principles of law, which has caused a certain confusion in relation to the law on State liability or responsibility for transboundary harm.

State Responsibility and Liability

For the past 20 years, the subject of State responsibility has been under study by the ILC, a UN body established to effect the codification and progressive development of international law. The issues involved are extremely complex and a detailed examination of them is beyond the scope of this study. The following is a very brief summary.

States are legally bound to observe the various rules and principles of international law found in the treaties to which they are party, in customary international law, in general principles of law and in the acts of international organisations which are binding upon them. The *doctrine of State responsibility* means that a State is *responsible* for a breach of international law. Such a breach is termed by the ILC as a "wrongful act". In other words, the State may be held accountable for its acts or omissions by the other State(s) involved or by the international community as a whole.

In all cases, a State committing a wrongful act will be required to cease the illegal behaviour, and in most cases, it will be liable to pay compensation, in a similar way as a company or individual would be for a breach of private law. However, the compensation for damage will be paid to the other States affected by the wrongful act, as a consequence of diplomatic negotiations or international litigation at the inter-State level. If a natural or legal person has been harmed by the illegal act of another State, his State of nationality may make a claim on his behalf to the State responsible. This is termed "diplomatic protection". In the latter case, the State will turn over the compensation to the victims. A State may claim for damage done to itself and to its nationals at the same time.

In its work on State responsibility, the ILC is studying the consequences of a breach of the law, rather than the substantive rules themselves. At an early stage, the Commission differentiated "State responsibility" from "international liability for the injurious consequences of acts not prohibited by international law". According to this latter theory, a State was subject to "international liability" in certain circumstances where it could be held liable to pay compensation for damage caused when no law had been violated. The types of situations envisaged are almost exclusively those involving transboundary damage to the environment and to human health caused by dangerous activities.

Some members of the Commission and some commentators deny the existence of a separate kind of "international liability", considering that so-called cases of liability are really just ordinary State responsibility. For, paradoxically, in

100

its work on international liability, the Commission has postulated a duty or responsibility to prevent harm, as well as an obligation to pay compensation for damage if harm is caused. Normally, where there is a legal obligation to prevent harm, responsibility for any damage caused results automatically, but certain States and members of the Commission are resisting this idea.

To a certain extent, the controversy resolves around the question whether States have an absolute duty to prevent transboundary harm or merely a duty to try to prevent it. The latter is referred to as an obligation of "due diligence", the requirement to take all possible care. In the first case, the liability would be strict, while in the second, States would be liable only if they do not take all the measures required to prevent any possible harm. The postulate of a "due diligence" obligation is a relatively new idea, supported largely by certain academics. The traditional rule was that of an absolute duty, albeit mitigated by circumstances. Some States believe that they should only be held liable if they have breached a particular rule laid down in a convention, or possibly in customary law.

State Responsibility for Transboundary Environmental Harm

Nevertheless, other States believe that the absolute duty to prevent transboundary harm is a general principle of international law independent of any particular rules set forth in international agreements or even customary international law. In the view of the States recognising the existence of the principle of State responsibility for transboundary harm, all States have a duty to preserve and protect the human environment; to prevent, reduce and control pollution in all sectors of the environment; and to ensure that activities within their jurisdiction or control do not cause damage in the territory of other States and to the global commons. This duty is owed directly to other States, as well as to the international community as a whole, including individuals wherever they may be, and to future generations.

The source of this duty, sometimes called the "no-harm principle", is fourfold. First, the duty not to cause harm to or in other States is a general principle of law derived from the fundamental tenets of the international legal and political system. Second, it is a general principle of law analogous to a principle found in national legal systems. Third, it is a principle of customary international law derived from conventional law and from the belief that the principle is legally binding. Fourth, it is a principle of conventional law expounded explicitly or implicitly in hundreds of bilateral or multilateral treaties.

The relevant principle of law is usually expressed in its Roman law formulation *sic utere tuo ut alienum non laedas* (use your own property in such a way as not to cause harm to the property of others). The principles of good neighbourliness, non-abuse of rights and good faith have been adduced in support of this general rule.

In international law, the corresponding principle may be logically deduced from the basic concepts of sovereignty, territorial integrity and sovereign equality. Just as every State has a right to respect for its sovereignty and territorial integrity, so must it respect equally the sovereignty and territorial integrity of other States. Furthermore, as sovereignty imparts the full authority and jurisdiction of the State to a certain territory, there is a concomitant duty to use that authority to ensure that activities within the State's jurisdiction do not cause harm or impinge upon the sovereignty or territorial integrity of other States. Damage to the environment or to human health in another State would be a clear breach of this rule.

This principle has been confirmed in two important international decisions on the issue of State responsibility for transboundary harm. In the *Trail Smelter Case (U.S.A. v. Canada),* the Arbitral Tribunal confirmed the obligation of States to prevent environmental damage beyond their borders from activities within their jurisdiction and their territory. In the words of the award:

> Under the principles of international law... no State has the right to use or to permit the use of its territory in such a manner as to cause injury by fumes in or to the territory of another or the properties or persons therein...

A few years later, the International Court of Justice reiterated the general principle in a case that did not involve the environment. In its judgement in the *Corfu Channel Case (U.K. v. Albania)*, the Court held that every State had an "obligation not to allow knowingly its territory to be used for acts contrary to the rights of other States".

At the 1972 Stockholm Conference on the Human Environment, the general principle received the approbation of all States in Principle 21 of the concluding Declaration. Although not binding itself, Principle 21 has become the locus classicus of the general international law on transboundary environmental harm. This seminal text reads as follows:

> States have in accordance with the Charter of the United Nations and the principles of international law, the sovereign right to exploit their own resources pursuant to their own environmental policies and the responsibility to ensure that activities within their jurisdiction and control do not cause damage to the environment of other States or of areas beyond the limits of national jurisdiction.

For the past 20 years, this expression of the common opinion of States has been confirmed as customary law through its inclusion in innumerable treaties and other binding legal instruments, as well as in further manifestations of what States consider the law to be, such as resolutions, declarations, guidelines, codes of conduct and sets of draft articles. Consequently, although interpretations may differ, it is clear that the international community has accepted Principle 21 as a general principle of international law and as a statement of the customary law evidenced in State practice.

One Responsibility Implies Another

Also addressed at Stockholm was the question of liability and compensation. In Principle 22, States pledged to co-operate to develop further the international law regarding liability and compensation of the victims of pollution and environmental damage caused by activities within the jurisdiction or control of States to areas beyond their jurisdiction. As noted above, in its work on State liability, the ILC has confirmed as a general principle of law that an actor who breaches an obligation will be held to account and will be subject to new obligations to cease the wrongful act and to perform the original obligation, as well as to restore the situation that would have prevailed had the breach not occurred, or if this is not possible, to compensate the victim.

These principles were declared unequivocally by the Permanent Court of International Justice in the *Chorzow Factory Case,* in 1928:

> [...] it is a principle of international law, and even a general conception of law, that any breach of an engagement involves an obligation to make reparation.

In relation to the responsibility of States to ensure that transboundary damage is not caused by activities within their jurisdiction, the concept is very simple: he who has the responsibility to control or supervise an installation or activity, also has the responsibility to ensure that the activity does no harm to others. Therefore, he must be held to account and must repair the damage or compensate the victim if harm does occur.

At least some of the contemporary confusion regarding responsibility and liability is linguistic. Whereas in English there are two different terms, in other languages the word "responsibility" encompasses four interrelated aspects of a total concept. Thus, "responsibility" means:

1. the care or control of a person, thing, installation or activity;

2. the obligation to ensure that the thing, activity, etc., does not cause harm to other persons, their property and the environment;

3. the obligation to be held to account if the previous obligation is breached; and

4. the obligation to repair the damage or to compensate the innocent victim.

In English, the term "liability" is used to refer to the third and fourth elements of the concept. Seen as a whole, the relationship between the responsibility to prevent damage and the responsibility to compensate the victims for any damage that may occur becomes quite evident.

Application to the Nuclear Field

In relation to nuclear activities, the responsibilities of the installation State are clear. While the operator is responsible for the daily, detailed operations of the installation or activity and for ensuring that it conforms to legal and regulatory requirements, the State under whose jurisdiction or control the installation or activity is operated is responsible for deciding to permit nuclear activities in the first place, for licensing the particular installation or activity, for enacting and enforcing safety legislation, for inspecting and monitoring the activity and its consequences, for making arrangements for emergency response, and generally for ensuring that it does not cause damage in the territory of other States or beyond the limits of national jurisdiction.

In fact, States are directly implicated in the development of nuclear activities, with many of them operating the activities themselves, or often subsidising them substantially. As noted in Chapter I, at the early stages of the establishment of nuclear industries, States intervened directly to encourage their development. Moreover, they regulate nuclear installations and activities much more stringently than they do any other type of dangerous activity.

Thus, the installation State is responsible for controlling the nuclear activities under its jurisdiction to other States and to the international community as a whole. Because the State has ultimate control over the activity, it may be considered internationally responsible and liable for any transboundary harm that may occur.

After the initial flurry of interest in State liability, the issue has been subsumed in the negotiations to revise the *Vienna Convention*. Although at present, there appears to be virtually no prospect of a convention on State liability being adopted, States accept the potential existence of such liability outside the context of the *Vienna Convention*. The current status of the negotiations is described in Chapter VIII.

Chapter VII

UNRESOLVED PROBLEMS

The *Joint Protocol* is only an interim solution to the problems in the civil liability system revealed by the accident at Chernobyl. In time, the Protocol may extend the system throughout Europe, east and west, so that victims in any State may claim compensation for damage caused by an accident in any other State. Yet, the other major problem remains. The existing civil liability conventions are inadequate, in part because the drafters at the time simply were not fully aware of certain possible consequences of an accident, and in part, because circumstances have changed since the early 1960's.

Improvements Required in the Civil Liability Conventions

Certain States parties and academic commentators have argued that both the *Paris* and the *Vienna Convention*s contain a number of shortcomings, the most important of which are noted below:

- insufficient coverage geographically;

- insufficient compensation;

- a too restrictive definition of "nuclear damage";

- overly brief time limits for the submission of claims;

- difficulties in the proof of causation and of damage;

- excessive exonerations and lack of provision for compensation if an exoneration applies;

- lack of priorities in the distribution of compensation;

- lack of harmonization between the two conventions and among the parties of each convention;

- military facilities are not expressly included;

- the difficulty and expense of private lawsuits conducted by individual victims;

- the inability of municipal courts to deal with possibly thousands of claimants, as well as with complex scientific and technical evidence;

- the lack of recognition of State responsibility for activities within a State's jurisdiction or control, and the corresponding incentive for States to ensure that their nuclear facilities are as safe as possible.

Geographical Scope

As explained in the previous section, after Chernobyl the *Joint Protocol* was adopted in the hope that the link between the *Paris* and *Vienna Conventions* would induce more States, especially the States of Central and Eastern Europe, to become parties to the *Vienna Convention*, as well as to the *Joint Protocol*, so that the scope of the civil liability regime would thereby be extended throughout all of Europe.

Even without the *Joint Protocol*, the *Paris Convention* expressly permits States parties to extend its benefits to non-member States. In the existing text of the *Vienna Convention*, however, there is no provision for such an extension. Therefore, except for cases in which parties to the *Paris Convention* have decided to extend its scope to non-parties, in the event of a nuclear accident in a State party to either convention, the regular rules of private international law would apply.

Amount of Compensation and Limitation of Liability

The greatest deficiencies of the current conventions are too low liability limits and insufficient compensation. From the billions of dollars worth of damage caused by Chernobyl, all countries recognised that there must be higher limits on liability. In fact, in some domestic legislation, the limits are much higher than the minimum limits in the conventions, while in a few, there are no limits at all. Yet, so-called "unlimited" liability is merely a statement of principle, not a practical possibility, as insurance cover is strictly limited, both in amount and in time. Furthermore, the confiscation of the assets of the operator would lead to a bankruptcy that may still not provide sufficient moneys for full compensation.

This problem of insufficiency was well understood even at the time of the negotiation of the original agreements, and was the reason for the conclusion of the *Brussels Convention*. However, there is no comparable system for providing additional compensation under the *Vienna Convention*. Even if limitations on the liability of the operator are raised to the limit of available insurance, some form of complementary funding will be required.

Furthermore, any fixed limits will rapidly become out of date. Therefore, some parties believe that a simplified means should be found to raise the liability limits periodically to take account of inflation and changes in the insurance market. Under the existing procedure, the Conventions would have to undergo a formal amendment, a procedure which could take several years to produce the desired effect. For example, the *Protocol Amending the Brussels Convention* was adopted in 1982, but only came into force in 1991.

Definition of Damage

At the time of the negotiation of the *Paris* and *Vienna Conventions*, it was envisaged that the type of damage caused by a nuclear accident would be limited to that suffered by individuals and legal entities: loss of life or personal injury, and loss of or damage to property. In the light of the experience of various types of industrial accidents, including oil and chemical spills, as well as nuclear incidents and disasters, it is now well understood that the range of potential damage is much broader. The movement of the cloud of radionuclides released at Chernobyl demonstrated that radioactive substances could spread over a far greater distance and for a longer time than previously imagined, and that economic loss or loss of profit as a result of contamination to the general environment, even in the absence of damage to property, could be substantial. Furthermore, most accidents will involve considerable costs of preventive or protective measures, possible further damage caused by preventive measures, the costs of cleaning up the contaminated area close to the site of the accident, and damage to the general environment, extending perhaps hundreds of kilometres from that site.

None of the above types of damages or costs is expressly mentioned in the civil liability conventions. Moreover, some of those costs and damages will be borne by the State, not by individuals. State agencies will introduce measures to protect the population immediately after the accident and as long as a danger exists; they will have to monitor the situation; to assist the sick and injured; to assess the damage; to try to clean up contaminated areas, and so forth. Damage to the environment is one of the most important heads of damage. As it is *res communis*, belonging to no one in particular and to everyone in general, only the State may claim for restoration or reparation, as it is responsible for the general welfare of the country and its people (*parens patriae*). At present, the conventions do not cover the costs of precautionary protective measures, such as evacuations, when the accident was averted or did not have any off-site effects.

In relation to damage to the environment, there has been some controversy in negotiations concerning non-nuclear conventions as to whether "impairment of the environment" or damage to the environment per se should be compensated and as to the most appropriate method of determining the amount of this compensation. For several years, it was accepted that apart from economic loss or loss of profit, compensation should be limited to the costs of reasonable measures of restoration undertaken or to be undertaken. Recently, however, there has been some movement towards allowing compensation for damage to the environment itself, even when restoration is impossible.

Proof of Causality and of Damage

No guidance is given in the civil liability conventions on the crucial issues of proof of causality and the level of contamination or kind of injury that is considered to constitute "nuclear damage". This is left to the discretion of the competent court applying national law.

Proof of causality is notoriously difficult to establish in the case of delayed damage resulting from exposure to relatively low levels of ionising radiation. From scientific research done primarily on Japanese victims of the Second World War, it is known that the extent of impairment of human health may not become apparent until decades after the accident, and that it may even affect the unborn.

While exposure beyond a certain threshold level produces immediate, well-known effects generally resulting in severe radiation sickness and death, lower levels of radiation produce subtle changes in body cells that may result in soft (leukaemia) or hard cancers after a latency period ranging from 3 to 30 years. Furthermore, when such cancers appear, they will be indistinguishable from cancers with other causes. Some means must be found to determine when such illnesses may be considered "nuclear damage". In some national law presumptions are made, but it would be preferable that the matter be regulated at the international level. (See the next section for more detail.)

Priorities

In the civil liability conventions, the distribution of compensation is left to the discretion of national courts. If there are insufficient funds to cover all the damage and if the court decides to distribute the available funds proportionally, then the result may be only partial compensation for those severely injured, while property damage that may not be a serious loss to the owner would be compensated to an equivalent proportion. Therefore, to ensure that compensation goes to the victims that need it most, some national laws establish priorities among the victims. Some States believe that provisions on priorities in the distribution of funds should be included in the conventions.

Time Limits for Submitting a Claim and Delayed Damage

Related to the questions of proof of causality, priorities, and insurance is the problem of too short time limits for making a claim. At present, the civil liability conventions provide for basic ten year limitation periods, whereas injuries such as radiation-induced cancers may not appear for up to 30 years after exposure. While in their national legislation (as is possible under the terms of the conventions), some States have extended the claims period to 30 years (the usual limit for damage claims), such a provision would not resolve all the associated problems.

First, insurance is not available to cover claims made more than ten years after the accident. In the national legislation that addresses this issues, compensation for damage manifested after the end of the limitation period is provided by the State. Second, there is the problem of distributing funds among early and late claimants. If the money available for compensation is distributed on a first-come, first-served basis, there may be little remaining for victims who become ill several decades after the accident. On the other hand, if payment is delayed until all the claims are judged, victims may have to wait many years to receive their compensation.

Exonerations

In the conventions, the operator is exonerated from liability if the damage was directly due to armed conflict, and may be exonerated if it is directly due to an exceptional natural disaster. In such cases, the victims may be left uncompensated. Most national laws provide for compensation from the State if operator liability is excluded by exonerations. Further, in many national laws, the sole exoneration is that of armed conflict, as the States concerned consider that nuclear installations should be built to withstand natural disasters and that if accidents do happen, the operator should bear the cost.

Military Installations

Liability for damage caused by accidents in military installations is not mentioned in the civil liability conventions. Nonetheless, some parties to the *Paris Convention* believe that military installations are covered. Others disagree. Many

States believe that military installations should be expressly included, as the damage from accidents in military installations may be as severe as that caused by civilian installations, the victims should not be left to bear the cost. As military installations are owned and operated by the State, compensation would have to be provided by the State.

Lack of Harmonization

There are a number of differences between the *Paris* and *Vienna Conventions*. If the *Vienna Convention* is revised as anticipated, the difference could become even greater. Furthermore, as the conventions leave many matters to the discretion of national legislation, there is a lack of harmonization even among the parties to the same conventions.

Competent Courts

As the civil liability conventions do not require that all actions in relation to any particular nuclear accident be instituted in the same court, victims may file claims in several different courts in the State having jurisdiction over the case. The results could be differences among decisions by the various courts in relation to criteria and standards in judgements, different compensation being granted for similar injuries, and perhaps, more compensation being awarded than funds available. (In relation to the *Paris Convention*, the OECD Steering Committee for Nuclear Energy has recommended that parties designate a single court to hear nuclear damage cases.)

Procedural Inadequacies of the Civil Liability System

For perhaps most potential claimants, the length, procedural complexity and the expenses involved in private lawsuits might present significant obstacles to obtaining compensation for nuclear damage. While the system of individual actions in the local courts may be adequate for the compensation for only a few victims suffering minor damage, the practical difficulties would be considerable in the event of a major nuclear accident causing damage to thousands of people in several different countries. As with the Chernobyl disaster, varying kinds and degrees of damage might be suffered by large numbers of people situated at a considerable distance from the site of the accident.

The victims may not be able to afford to hire the lawyers, the scientific experts, the technologists and translators necessary to conduct an action for damages that would take place in a foreign court, under a foreign legal system, in a foreign language and in a country perhaps thousands of kilometres distant from their homes. Furthermore, the proceedings might take a decade to conclude and most of the compensation might go to pay legal fees and other expenses. (For those who are successful, legal costs awarded by the court would be paid by the operator.)

In addition, if all nuclear liability actions relating to one incident were consolidated into a single national court, as would be necessary to avoid inconsistent judgments, that court might be faced with the difficulty of handling thousands of individual claims. Finally, national judges would likely lack the expertise to understand the complex scientific, technical, and medical issues involved. (In contrast, if the claims were to be judged by an international tribunal or commission, the judges could be especially chosen for their expertise.)

Action at the IAEA

It was the recognition of these and other problems in the existing instruments during the *crise de conscience* after Chernobyl, that led many States to call for a thorough review of the civil liability system and for the revision of the *Vienna Convention* or the conclusion of an entirely new convention. The question of the revision of the civil liability system was set aside temporarily during the preparation of the *Joint Protocol*. Following the adoption of the Protocol in September 1988, the Member States of the IAEA decided to embark upon negotiations to modernise the international regime of liability and compensation for nuclear damage. The current status of the negotiations is described in Chapter VIII.

Intervention Levels and the Proof of Damage

The Problem

As noted above, no guidance is given in the civil liability conventions on the questions of causality and the level of contamination and the precise kind of injury that should be considered as "nuclear damage". Furthermore, the conventions do not even mention the issue of compensation for protective or preventive measures. After Chernobyl, the Soviet Union insisted that the emissions of radioactive material from the stricken plant that had reached other countries were not dangerous, that the protective measures were unnecessary, and that all the consequential damage or economic loss was therefore caused by the action of other governments. This was one of the reasons given by the USSR for denying liability.

Essentially, the first question is: which levels of radioactivity in the human body pose a danger to health, and the second, which levels of radioactivity in food and the environment will result in these dangerous levels in the human body? The third question is which protective measures should be taken in which circumstances to most effectively prevent dangerous levels of radioactivity from being absorbed by humans? Clearly, if the measures taken by governments or by individuals are not necessary to prevent damage in view of the prevailing level of radioactivity, a claim for compensation will not be allowed.

Therefore, before decisions can be taken concerning compensation for preventive measures, as well as for further damage caused by preventive measures, it would be helpful if States could agree upon which levels of radioactivity are hazardous to human health, which levels of contamination in food and in the environment will lead to those hazardous levels, and which protective measures will be appropriate in which circumstances. Without such international agreement, a court would have to make its own decision, based either upon possibly conflicting expert evidence, or upon national intervention levels.

The result may be a decision that is unacceptable to some of the countries suffering the damage. For, without international agreement, a level of radioactivity that was considered safe in one country might be considered as dangerous in another. If the national intervention levels in the country of the court having jurisdiction are fairly high, then foreign victims might be denied compensation which in their own country would be compensated. The country concerned might then be moved to intervene on the victims' behalf. If there were damage in several countries with different intervention levels, the result could be international disputes between the various countries involved.

The same kind of consensus on dangerous levels of radioactivity would be necessary to determine when property is so contaminated that it can no longer be used and must therefore be considered as eligible for compensation. For example, persons who have been evacuated from their homes or places of work may not be able to return to them if they are contaminated by radioactivity above a certain level. International agreement on the relevant level would greatly assist a court in determining whether to award compensation for the loss of the property concerned.

In relation to personal injury and the impairment of health, the problem is even more complex. As already noted, relatively high levels of exposure above a certain threshold cause certain characteristic radiation illnesses that appear within a short time of exposure. The higher the exposure, the more severe the injury. As these illnesses, termed "deterministic effects", are readily recognisable, there should be no difficulty in determining that compensation is payable.

On the other hand, lower levels of exposure to radiation cause minute modifications of body cells, that in time may or may not result in disease or illness. Although these so-called "stochastic effects"are assumed to have no threshold, the probability of illness is assumed to increase with the amount of dose. The latency period for stochastic effects ranges from a few years for leukemia to several decades for solid tumours. Since the cancers caused by ionising radiation exactly resemble those caused by other factors, it is virtually impossible to prove that any particular cancer was caused by any particular nuclear accident, especially if several decades have passed since the exposure.

As a consequence, in order to avoid denying recovery to victims suffering stochastic effects, some means will have to be found to link exposures to ionising radiation in certain circumstances to certain specific illnesses. In the alternative, people could be compensated for merely being exposed to hazardous levels of radiation. In such circumstances, compensation could be made on the basis of presumptions or a balance of probabilities. In order to avoid international disputes over the compensation awarded after a nuclear accident, such a determination should preferably involve an international agreement involving a political decision made on a scientific basis.

Protective Measures and Intervention Levels

Protective Measures

When a nuclear accident occurs, every State that may be affected will have to decide what steps to take to protect its population from the hazards of the ionising radiation that may be emitted by the nuclear installation in which the accident has occurred. For the most effective response, contingency plans should contain provisional measures to be implemented before the nature and extent of the accident is known. Then, once more precise information is available, from national and international monitoring of levels of radioactivity in the environment, States will adopt the specific protective measures that are most appropriate and effective for the prevailing circumstances in the specific areas in question. The term "protective measures" refers to any action taken in response to a nuclear accident that has occurred, or is in imminent danger of occurring, in order to prevent or minimise damage from ionising radiation, especially the protection of life and human health.

In response to the threat of contamination from the cloud of radioactive particles produced by the accident at Chernobyl, governments of affected States in Europe took a wide variety of measures of varying magnitude in order to protect their populations. In some States nothing at all was done, while in others counter-measures were fairly restrictive, causing considerable disruption in every day life and resulting in significant economic costs. The duration of the measures also varied substantially. The lack of harmonization in national standards was embarrassingly evident, contributing not a little to the anxiety of the population, and lending some credence to the Soviet contentions that the actions were unwarranted.

While the variation in response can be explained in part by the differences in contamination levels, by the characteristics of particular environments, and by different dietary habits, it is also true that there were important national differences in the choice of intervention levels, as well as in systems for radiation protection and public health. Furthermore, the available international guidance was not entirely consistent and was deficient in that it was applicable only to the "near-field" situation close to the site of the accident and to the short term. Before Chernobyl, it was not expected that the effects of an accident would be so widespread and of such a long duration.

Intervention Levels

The type of protective measure adopted depends both on the relevant circumstances of the situation and on the *primary intervention* and derived intervention levels applied. A primary intervention level is the quantity of a dose of radiation to individuals, which, if exceeded or predicted to be exceeded in an accident, requires the application of a given protective action. A *derived intervention level* is the activity concentration in a given environmental matrix or foodstuff which, under certain assumptions, corresponds to a dose to individuals equal to the primary intervention level. The application of protective measures such as sheltering, evacuation, the administration of prophylactic doses of iodine, and the banning of contaminated foodstuffs are directly dependent upon the relevant intervention levels.

Problems may arise from differences in national intervention levels, as in one country a small dose of radiation may be deemed to be dangerous and to require the banning of foodstuffs, while in another, a greater dose may be considered safe, and no protective measures will be taken. The result could be confusion and even fear in the populations concerned. Furthermore, because of the amount of food and other goods moving in international trade, the repercussions on imports (and exports) would obviously be quite considerable, with imports of goods considered to be contaminated by the importing country being prohibited, while the exporting country may believe they are perfectly innocuous.

114

Before Chernobyl, intervention levels were based upon the ICRP *Recommendations of 1977* and the *1982 Basic Safety Standards* jointly developed and issued by the IAEA, the NEA, the World Health Organisation (WHO) and the International Labour Organisation (ILO). Due to the large variety of administrative, social and environmental conditions existing in various countries, these standards expressly stipulate that the establishment of intervention levels for particular circumstances, including nuclear emergencies, is the responsibility of national authorities.

Despite the understanding that the establishment of intervention levels was a national responsibility, differences in those levels in neighbouring countries were soon perceived as a problem, and initiatives were taken by several international organisations towards the adoption of recommendations to promote a common interpretation and a coherent approach. The IAEA, the EEC, the ICRP, the WHO and the NEA, all provided guidance.

The recommendations of the various organisations were largely homogeneous. As a matter of general principle, they take the approach that the social cost of a countermeasure should be less than the detriment that it is intended to prevent. The method adopted is based on defining an accident and appropriate countermeasures, and identifying a range of radioactive doses between a high level, at which protection measures should be taken, and a lower level, below which countermeasures are not warranted.

Nevertheless, significant differences remained in the guidance given for the establishment of ranges of dose in the recommendations of the ICRP, the IAEA, the EEC, and the WHO. It was these differences that were primarily responsible for the considerable divergence in precautions taken throughout Europe after the Chernobyl disaster. As a consequence, the responsible international organisations realised that efforts had to be made to further clarify and better harmonize the general criteria for the management of protective response to accidents having transfrontier consequences.

Therefore, immediately after Chernobyl, work began towards a unified approach to radiation protection in the case of accidental exposure. Since 1986, the NEA and the IAEA have been working on the problem of intervention levels and protective measures, while the WHO and the FAO have been working on safety levels for radioactivity in food, both in relation to national production and consumption and in relation to food moving in international trade. Simultaneously, the European Community has developed its own intervention levels with respect to food and foodstuffs.

Since 1990, a new Inter-Agency Committee on Radiation Safety has sponsored the development of revised *Basic Safety Standards* (BSS) based on recent research and the latest 1991 recommendations of the ICRP. To oversee the creation of the new BSS, the IACRS has established a Joint Secretariat comprised of the agencies involved in the 1982 version, plus the FAO and the Pan-American Health Organisation. The new BSS provide guidance on intervention levels and protective measures.

Once the new standards are adopted, the question becomes whether and how this guidance might be used in relation to determining the amount of compensation to be awarded to victims and for what kinds of injury or damage.

Damage Caused by Radioactive Waste

The question of liability for damage caused by the disposal of radioactive waste is not expressly addressed in either the *Paris* or the *Vienna Conventions*. Although both Conventions expressly cover the storage and transport of waste, facilities for the final disposal of radioactive waste are not specifically listed in the definition of a nuclear installation. Consequently, the question has arisen whether the existing conventions may be applied to nuclear damage arising from waste disposal. In the context of the *Paris Convention*, the question was partly answered in 1984. In relation to the *Vienna Convention*, no decision has been made.

Factual Background

Radioactive waste is produced during all phases of the nuclear fuel cycle, primarily during the operation and dismantling of nuclear power plants and research reactors, but also from the use of radioisotopes in medicine, industry and agriculture. Different types of radioactive wastes pose health hazards at different levels depending upon the concentration of the radioactive substance (specific activity) and the length of time taken for the radioactivity to decay to safe levels (measured in half-lives).

Low-level wastes are both low in the level of radioactivity and relatively short in the duration of toxicity – from several days to several centuries, while high level wastes such as spent fuel and wastes from reprocessing are characterised by relatively high levels of radioactivity and may remain toxic for up to several million years. Furthermore, high level wastes emit a significant amount of heat.

Because of the level and duration of their toxicity, the fundamental principle for the disposal of radioactive wastes is isolation from the biosphere for as long as the wastes in question pose an unacceptable risk for human beings and their environment. This isolation is effected by special containers as well as by a succession of barriers, including the natural environment immediately surrounding the repository itself. The disposal may be effected either on land or in the sea; however, as sea disposal of solid waste ceased in 1982, in future radioactive wastes may be eliminated exclusively on land.

For the purposes of final disposal, low level, short-lived wastes are usually placed in shallow land burial sites, specially engineered structures or abandoned mines. Due to the relatively short half-lives of this kind of waste, the expected life-time of near-surface repositories is up to 300 years. Because of the longer half-life and greater activity of the nuclides in high-level waste, this disposal is expected to be effected in repositories located in deep, stable geological formations with an isolation period of from tens of thousands to millions of years. The exact methods and administrative arrangements for waste disposal, as well as the governing laws and regulations will vary from country to country, but they are all largely based on the same principles.

Disposal of Wastes from Nuclear Installations

When nuclear substances are no longer used, they are first conditioned and then held in interim storage until a disposal facility becomes available. This storage may last for several decades and up to 100 years if necessary. It is an integral component of the operation of a nuclear installation and clearly belongs to the third party liability régime of the *Paris* and *Vienna Conventions*.

Once a disposal facility has been constructed, there will be an operational phase during which waste is continually or periodically placed in the repository. The filling of the disposal facility may last for several decades. This operational phase is usually termed the "pre-closure phase".

Then, in the "post-closure" phase, all activity will cease and the repository will be closed. Thereafter, in the case of shallow land burial, engineered structures or other near-surface repositories for low level wastes, unauthorised access to the site will have to be prevented, buildings may have to be maintained, and the environment will have to be monitored for radioactivity levels. This surveillance will continue until the radioactivity of the wastes has decayed to a safe level, up to 300 years.

In the case of deep geological disposal, notably for high level wastes, following closure, the safety of the installation will be assured by purely passive features – a succession of barriers, both constructed and geological – to prevent the escape of radioactive material. Therefore, because of the remoteness of and difficult access to the waste, it should be sufficient to provide for the maintenance of appropriate records of the site's existence and location, to prevent any activity on the site that might disturb the repository or inadvertent human intrusion.

Most radioactive waste is now being held in interim storage, awaiting arrangements for final disposal. However, a few repositories for low level, short-lived waste are in operation or under construction. It is expected that the first repositories for the disposal of high level waste may commence operations by the beginning of the next century.

Application of the Liability Conventions

Paris Convention

Apparently, the *Paris Convention* was not drafted with the case of radioactive waste disposal specifically in mind. In the definition of nuclear installations, facilities for storage are listed, but the status of repositories for final disposal is left unclear.

In 1984, the NEA Group of Experts on Third Party Liability addressed the question of liability arising from the disposal of nuclear substances. The group distinguished between the "pre-closure" and "post-closure" phases of disposal, deciding to set aside consideration of the latter for the time being, as it was not an immediate problem. In relation to the pre-closure phase, the Experts considered that the activities involved were closely linked to and were sufficiently similar to the operations of the other stages of the fuel cycle to warrant its inclusion in the regular third party liability system.

Accordingly, upon a recommendation of the Group of Experts, the OECD Steering Committee for Nuclear Energy adopted a Decision on 11 April 1984 stating that:

> Installations for the disposal of nuclear substances shall, for the pre-closure phase, be considered as "nuclear installations" within the meaning of Article 1 (a)(ii) of the *Paris Convention*.

As a consequence, it is now clear that all the provisions of the *Paris Convention* apply to a disposal facility during its pre-closure phase.

In taking its Decision, the Steering Committee did not wish to prejudge the question whether or not the *Paris Convention* also applies to the post-closure phase. If the *Paris Convention* does not apply, there is no international legal regime governing liability for damage caused during the post-closure phase, and national law alone will apply.

In 1993, the question of liability in relation to the final disposal of radioactive waste was again raised within the NEA Group of Governmental Experts. The Group is now considering whether the time is appropriate to address the issue of liability for damage caused by the disposal of radioactive waste in the post-closure phase. If it is, it will need to consider whether an international regime is necessary, and if so, of what kind, and in what type of instrument it should be given effect, e.g. the *Paris Convention*, a new convention, a decision, or a recommendation. The answer may not be reached for some time, and may depend upon the course of the revisions of the existing conventions

Certain aspects of the post-closure phase of a radioactive waste repository are very different from the type of situation envisaged by the drafters of the *Paris Convention*. The nature of the risk is not the same as that associated with an operating power plant, nor with a waste facility in the pre-closure phase, since there is no longer any operational activity within the facility itself. Sudden accidents causing large releases of radiation become much less likely, and the risk is rather of gradual contamination of the environment, which may remain undetected for some time.

Because of the length of time during which the waste will remain radioactive, the provisions regarding insurance or financial security in the liability conventions would not be appropriate for the post-closure phase. Furthermore, insurance companies are reluctant to provide cover for a "continuous occurrence", as opposed to a sudden event. The limitation period for bringing claims of ten or even thirty years from the date of the incident would also need reconsideration. In addition, the time-frame involved affects the nature of the operator – which will most likely need to be a government or government agency – and the nature of the control exercised by the operator.

In addition, the Group of Governmental Experts is considering whether the 1984 Decision provides a complete solution in relation to the pre-closure phase. In particular, it is expected to examine whether, in the light of developments over the last decade in the technical approach to radioactive waste disposal, the division between the "pre-closure" and "post-closure" phases needs further definition or refinement.

Vienna Convention

Like the *Paris Convention*, the *Vienna Convention* covers facilities for the processing of nuclear substances and their storage, but does not expressly cover installations for the final disposal of radioactive wastes. However, the *Vienna*

Convention does not at present confer on any body a power analogous to that which the Steering Committee for Nuclear Energy has to determine that particular facilities are to be considered to be "installations" for the purposes of the *Paris Convention*. Therefore the status of waste repositories under the *Vienna Convention* remains unspecified. The issue of liability for damage caused by the disposal of radioactive waste has been mentioned, but not so far discussed, during the negotiations to revise the *Vienna Convention*. However, one of the proposed revisions to the *Vienna Convention* is the addition of the following new sub-paragraph to the definition of "installation":

> (iv) such other installations in which there are nuclear fuel or radioactive products or waste as the Board of Governors shall time to time determine.

It is possible that this provision, if adopted, will in the future lead to a determination by the Board of Governors concerning the application of the *Vienna Convention* to facilities for the final disposal of radioactive waste.

Chapter VIII

THE MODERNISATION OF THE NUCLEAR LIABILITY REGIME

Negotiations in Progress at the IAEA

Once the *Joint Protocol* was adopted, attention turned again to the questions of the revision of the *Vienna Convention* and the need for a convention on State liability. While the *Joint Protocol* was being adopted, at its 1988 meeting, the IAEA General Conference requested the Board of Governors "to continue", as a matter of priority, "consideration of the question of liability for damage arising from a nuclear accident", and "to convene in 1989 an open-ended working group to study all aspects of liability for nuclear damage".

At its meeting in February 1989, the Board of Governors therefore established the open-ended working group. At its first meeting the Group identified for further consideration a number of issues relating to both civil and State liability, while at the second, the Group discussed these issues and considered possible improvements to the civil liability system. In its report to the Board of Governors at the end of 1989, the Working Group recommended that its mandate be transferred to a new Standing Committee for Nuclear Damage.

In February 1990, the Board accepted this recommendation, transforming the existing Standing Committee on Civil Liability for Nuclear Damage (established pursuant to the *Vienna Convention*), by dropping the qualifier "civil", into a new committee with the responsibility to:

"(i) consider international liability for nuclear damage, including international civil liability, international State liability, and the relationship between international civil and State liability;

(ii) keep under review problems relating to the *Vienna Convention on Civil Liability for Nuclear Damage* and advise States party to the Convention on any such problems..."

and to prepare for a conference to revise the *Vienna Convention*.

Participating in the negotiations are around fifty States, a number of intergovernmental organisations, including the Commission of the European Communities (CEC), the OECD Nuclear Energy Agency, the United Nations Environment Programme (UNEP), the Food and Agricultural Organisation (FAO) and the African-Asian Legal Consultative Committee; plus three non-governmental organisations: the European Insurance Committee, Greenpeace International and the International Union of Producers and Distributors of Electrical Energy (UNIPEDE). As one might expect, these various participants have different interests and sometimes divergent goals.

Differences exist on a number of specific issues. Less developed States with nuclear power programmes may tend to favour a fairly low liability limit, as may those with less developed insurance industries. Conversely, wealthier States with a flourishing nuclear industry and a robust insurance sector may tend to favour higher limits. In relation to military facilities, some States with such installations do not wish them to be included, while other States believe that the revised *Vienna Convention* should expressly cover military facilities, to ensure that the victims of accidents in such facilities are not denied compensation.

Added to the complex political and economic issues and a multiplicity of points of view depending on whether a State has a nuclear power programme or not, is developing or industrialised, is the problem of legal differences. For, each State has its own legal system and therefore its own, perhaps unique, method of approaching the question of civil liability. Despite the unanimity on the general principle of strict liability, there are genuine differences on matters such as the damage to be covered and the setting of priorities in the payment of claims.

In considering the proposals for revision outlined in this chapter, the reader should bear in mind the unresolved problems noted in Chapter VII and the related provisions in some national laws described in Chapter V.

Subjects under Discussion

The discussions in the Standing Committee have focused on three main subjects:

– Amendments to the *Vienna Convention*;

– Supplementary Funding; and

– State Liability and its Relationship to Civil Liability.

Under consideration are a number of draft texts for the revision of the *Vienna Convention*, none of which has been definitely adopted, although there is general agreement on a few. However, in respect of some proposals, it may take some more time to arrive at a consensus. In relation to supplementary funding, two draft conventions somewhat similar to the *Brussels Convention* have been under consideration. Although some States would have preferred to postpone any further discussion on them until after work on the *Vienna Convention* is completed, these conventions are now being reviewed in parallel with the draft amendments to the *Vienna Convention*. The issue of supplementary funding will be examined in Chapter IX. On State liability, little has been said and less has been agreed.

Amendments to the *Vienna Convention*

The main points addressed have been:

- geographical scope;

- including military facilities;

- increasing the amount of liability for the operator;

- updating the liability limit;

- extending the time limits for the submission of claims;

- extending the definition of nuclear damage to include damage to the environment, preventive measures and loss of profit;

- establishing an international claims commission;

- representation by States of their nationals;

- establishing priorities for the payment of compensation;

- restricting exonerations;

- settlement of disputes; and

- various technical adjustments.

After a lengthy process of consideration of numerous proposals on almost every conceivable issue, a core set of texts that had not been rejected were polished into draft articles at the Seventh Meeting of the Standing Committee for Nuclear Damage. The amendments are in the form of a draft protocol ready to be submitted to a diplomatic conference. Although wide agreement was reached in the Drafting Committee on most of the wording of the articles, fundamental disagreement remains on whether some of them should be adopted at all.

The following is a factual commentary on the proposals made and the State of the negotiations at the time of publication, after the Ninth Negotiating Session in May 1994.

Geographical Scope

Usually, a convention applies only between or among the States that are party to it. That is, it will be effective on the territory, including the territorial sea, and in relation to the persons, over which the State has jurisdiction. Nevertheless, it is possible for States to agree to provide the benefits of their convention to other States that are not parties to it.

At present, the *Vienna Convention* contains no provision on geographical scope. However, it is generally accepted that the Convention applies to all damage suffered in States parties from a nuclear accident for which an operator of a State party is liable. Damage suffered on and over the high seas by persons and property under the jurisdiction of a contracting party is also covered. In order not to discriminate against victims in non-parties and to ensure that the Convention regime is applied uniformly to all victims, it has been proposed to include a new article to extend coverage to include damage suffered in non-contracting States.

However, some States have objected to the idea of extending the benefits of the Convention to non-parties, without receiving anything in return. As a compromise, a proposed article has been drafted which declares that the Convention applies to nuclear damage, wherever suffered, with the proviso that installation States may exclude the application of the convention to damage suffered in the territory or exclusive economic zone (EEZ) of a non-contracting State, but only if that State has a nuclear installation in its territory or EEZ, and does not afford equivalent reciprocal benefits.

Some States consider the proviso to be unduly restrictive, while others object to the article on principle.

Military Installations

Military installations are not mentioned in either the *Paris* or the *Vienna Convention*. Nevertheless, some *Paris Convention* States believe that they may be included, because they are not expressly excluded, while others disagree. On the other hand, warships are covered by the *Convention on the Liability of the Operators of Nuclear Ships*, which may be one reason why the Convention is not yet in force. For, some States object to the inclusion of military facilities or equipment in any kind of private law or liability regime. On the other hand, since military installations may cause as much damage as civilian ones, other States strongly favour expressly including military installations in the revised *Vienna Convention* regime.

Under discussion is a proposed new article stating that the Convention applies to all nuclear installations, whether peaceful or not, with the option of a contracting party being able to declare that military installations are not covered. If such a declaration is made, however, the State must ensure that the victims of a nuclear accident are compensated "at a level not less than would be provided if the Convention applied". The latter formulation is similar in substance to that used for the exclusion of military vessels from requirements in maritime conventions regarding safety and pollution prevention (the *Brussels Supplementary Convention* also contains a provision of this nature). Although the draft formulation of an article has been agreed, some States are still strongly opposed to the inclusion of military installations in the revised convention.

To cover the case of a military installation situated on the territory of a State party, but operated by a State that is not a party, a further provision stipulates that the Convention will not apply to such installations, unless otherwise provided by the legislation of the State party.

Amount of Liability

Although one of the primary reasons for revising the *Vienna Convention* was to increase the amount of compensation available for the victims, thus far, exact figures for new liability limits have scarcely been discussed. However, there is a proposal to replace the current amount with a limit of "not less than 150 million Special Drawing Rights" (SDRs). All States have agreed to adopt the SDR as the unit of account. The figure 150 million derives from a recommendation by the OECD Steering Committee for Nuclear Energy that this amount be used by the *Paris Convention* States. The sum is based upon what is generally available under nuclear liability insurance in such countries. However, in the case of a lesser risk, a lower limit (as yet unspecified), will be permitted, provided that the installation State ensures that public funds are available to compensate for damage up to the general liability limit. The liability limit set by a State applies to an accident for which one of its operators is liable, wherever the accident occurs. As in the existing text, the liability limit would remain exclusive of court costs and interest.

It is possible that the new limit of liability will not be decided until the very last minute, at the diplomatic conference held to finalise the text and to adopt the convention.

Updating the Liability Limit

Due to inflation and other factors, such as changes in the insurance market, it is anticipated that the liability limit may have to be updated from time to time in the future. In order to avoid having to undergo a lengthy amending process each time, a more rapid procedure to amend the liability limit has been proposed. A new article would permit a meeting to be convened to amend the liability limits if requested by one-third of the States parties. If the amendments are approved by a two-thirds majority of those present and voting, with at least half the parties being present, then the amendments will be notified to all the States parties.

At the end of a six month waiting period, the amendments will be considered to be accepted, unless one-third of the parties object. Twelve months after the acceptance, the amendment will enter into force for all parties that have not objected. This procedure avoids the usual protracted delay while parties ratify an amending protocol and places the onus on parties who do not wish an amendment to object. If objections are not made by two-thirds of the parties, then those States who have done nothing are automatically bound by the revised limit. On the other hand, the objectors will not be so bound, and they are free to maintain the lower limits already existing in their national law.

This sort of "tacit acceptance" procedure has been used in a number of existing conventions, especially those dealing with marine pollution and maritime safety. However, some States feel uneasy about being bound without their having given their express consent.

Time Limits

In the proposed amendments, the old time limit for the submission of claims of ten years from the date of the accident is replaced by a thirty year limit for loss of life and personal injury, with ten years being retained for all other damage. However, if under national law the liability of the operator is covered by financial security, including State funds, for a longer period, the operator may remain liable for such longer period. Actions brought after ten years from the date of the accident shall not affect the rights to compensation of any person who has brought an action before the expiry of the ten year period.

This longer limit for personal injuries corresponds to the usual limit in most national laws and is much more favourable to the victim than the old ten year rule. For, most cancers resulting from exposure to ionising radiation do not become manifest until from a few years to a few decades after the exposure.

A new paragraph regarding the "discovery rule" provides that the right to compensation under the Convention shall be extinguished if an action is not brought within three years of the date the victim knew or ought reasonably to have had knowledge of the damage and of the operator liable, provided that the basic limitation periods of thirty or ten years are not exceeded. This provision effects greater harmonization than the existing one, which merely permitted an extinction period of "not less than three years".

The Concept of Nuclear Damage

In relation to the definition of nuclear damage, the existing text was clearly inadequate as it covered only damage to persons and to property. Neither damage to the environment nor preventive measures were included. Therefore, the negotiators proposed to follow the model set in a number of recent conventions dealing with liability for environmental damage in other fields. In the draft under discussion, environmental damage would be compensated, but only in relation to economic loss caused by damage to the environment, or the "costs of reasonable measures of reinstatement undertaken or to be undertaken".

The draft definitions are not yet settled and are fairly controversial, but after the eighth negotiating session in October 1993, nuclear damage was defined as meaning, in addition to the loss of life and personal injury and the loss of or damage to property already covered: impairment of the environment, "unless insignificant" or "unless at tolerable levels"; loss of profit from impairment of the environment and other loss of profit ("pure economic loss") if and to the extent determined by the national court; and the costs of preventive measures and further loss or damage caused by preventive measures.

Compensation for impairment of the environment would be limited to any "reasonable measures" aiming to reinstate or restore damaged or destroyed components of the environment, or to introduce, where reasonable, the equivalent of these components to the environment. The law of the State where the damage is suffered would determine who was entitled to take such measures.

Loss of profit related to personal injury or damage to property will be covered in accordance with the provisions of national law. Under the current proposal, impairment of the environment that gives rise to loss of profit would also be compensated. However, there may be some difficulty in determining exactly what would be loss of profit arising from impairment of the environment. For example, if contamination of the air, soil and water rendered a farmer's produce unfit to eat, so that the authorities ordered it destroyed, the loss might be considered as resulting either from impairment of the environment, or from damage to property, if the crops could be considered the farmer's property.

127

Rather more difficult is the question of compensation for measures of reinstatement of the environment. Who would be entitled to take such measures, and which measures might be considered "reasonable"? The same questions apply to compensation for preventive measures, which measures would qualify for compensation and who would be entitled to take them? Some obvious measures that should be compensated are evacuation of the population from areas that are contaminated or that might become so, and the banning from sale of contaminated foodstuffs.

Also included in the draft is a reference to so-called "pure economic loss". The qualification "pure" means that the economic loss in question is not the direct consequence of personal injury or damage to property. An example of pure economic loss would be a reduction in tourism due to nuclear contamination or fear of nuclear contamination. After Chernobyl, there were extensive cancellations of holidays in Europe, especially in the former USSR and Eastern Europe. Although this type of loss has regularly been awarded in certain oil pollution cases, in many countries compensation for pure economic loss is not available. Consequently, some States are opposed to the inclusion of the provision. Others consider the provision to be "overly broad". As a compromise, in the current draft, the issue is left to the national courts to decide.

The new definition of a nuclear incident would include the imminent threat of an incident. This change was proposed as the existing text would permit claims for preventive measures taken only *after* an accident had actually occurred. That is, the costs of an evacuation would not be covered if it took place before a release of radioactivity actually occurred or when an accident was ultimately averted. With the inclusion of an imminent threat in the definition of an incident, the costs of a precautionary evacuation would be compensated under the revised convention.

Despite the lengthy discussions on the issue of the extension of the concept of nuclear damage to embrace damage to the environment, the cost of preventive measures, etc., much remains to be done. While perhaps most States favour compensating more of the damage and losses occasioned by an accident, many also realise that there may not be sufficient funds available to compensate everyone. If that is so, then the amount of compensation due to each victim will have to be reduced. Some States do not wish to see damage to the environment being compensated when individuals may have to bear a portion of their own loss for personal injury and damage to property.

To a certain extent, the answer to this conundrum will depend on the amount of funding finally available, including whether the moneys resulting from the liability of the operator will be supplemented from other sources.

Some States would prefer an internationalised procedure to deal with claims for damages following a nuclear accident with international implications. Given the material limitations of domestic courts, it might be difficult for them to deal with possibly thousands of foreign claimants, who would not understand the system, who would require translators and interpreters, and so forth. Furthermore, some of the claimants might be doubtful about the impartiality of the court having jurisdiction, if it is the national court of the defendant, as would be the case of an accident occurring in a nuclear installation. Consequently, a number of countries have proposed including in the revised *Vienna Convention* the possibility of establishing an "International Claims Commission".

A new article would provide an optional claim settlement procedure in the form of an International Claims Commission which the installation State and one or more contracting parties affected by the nuclear incident in question may decide to establish. The Claims Commission would enjoy exclusive jurisdiction over claims emanating from persons within the jurisdiction of the countries establishing it. This process would operate in parallel with claims brought in the competent municipal court by other parties or persons suffering nuclear damage.

To ensure that all the moneys available for compensation are distributed by a single body, it would be stipulated that the court having jurisdiction should determine the distribution, while accepting as definitive any decision of the Claims Commission. The latter would apply both the provisions of the *Vienna Convention* and the law of the municipal court. The composition of the Claims Commission would be agreed by the parties participating and the procedures would be based upon those of a generally accepted code on commercial arbitration.

States not involved in the establishment of the Claims Commission, including non-contracting States if damage suffered within their territory is covered by the Convention, may subsequently submit to its jurisdiction. If they do so and agree to pay part of the cost, then the exclusive jurisdiction of the Commission would apply to actions regarding claims for damage caused by the nuclear accident brought by any victim within their territory. States opposed to the concept of an International Claims Commission have pointed out that its establishment would create a duplication of jurisdiction between the Claims Commission and the national court, with a consequent possibility of inconsistent judgements.

Representation by States

One of the problems of all civil liability regimes is that many people, especially those who have suffered extensive personal injury or property damage, would be unable to afford the trouble and expense of instituting a lawsuit in order to pursue a claim for damages. In order to assist such persons making claims in foreign jurisdictions, some commentators have called for them to be represented by their State of nationality, which would present the claim on their behalf. A draft new article embodies a proposal entitling actions to be brought by contracting parties on behalf of and with the consent of victims suffering damage who are their citizens or who are resident or domiciled in their territory.

In the case of the chemical accident at Bhopal, the Indian government pursued such a procedure after adopting legislation giving it the exclusive right to represent the claimants in the courts. The victims were obviously in no position to enforce their rights themselves. Since, in the event of a nuclear accident, it is likely that States would wish to submit claims themselves for damage to the environment, for clean-up costs, for damage to State property and for preventive measures, it would be convenient for claims by individuals and companies to be presented by the State at the same time as its own.

Priorities in the Distribution of Compensation

If there is a limitation on the liability of the operator, it is possible that there will not be sufficient funds available to compensate all the damage arising from a nuclear accident. As a consequence, some system of equitable distribution of the compensation available could be considered desirable. For example, the funds may be distributed proportionately, with each victim only receiving a percentage of the total sum of his loss.

However, this solution would mean placing equal value on claims regarding personal injury and claims regarding damage to property, with the result that some relatively unimportant property claims would be partially compensated, while individuals would have to bear some of their losses due to death and personal injury. In some States, as this result was considered inequitable, national legislation stipulates that compensation of claims for loss of life and personal injury shall be given priority over those for damage to property.

In the existing conventions, the equitable distribution of the funds available for compensation is determined by the law of the Court having jurisdiction. However, in the interests of both uniformity and fairness to the victims, a number of States wish to include a system of priorities in the revised *Vienna Convention*. Although some favoured a precise numerical formula, differences of opinion have resulted in a provision simply stating that where the claims exceed or are likely to exceed the liability of the operator, priority in the distribution of compensation shall be given to claims in respect of loss of life or personal injury. Without a precise formula, the court would have greater flexibility in its determination of which claims should have priority.

Some States are opposed in principle to the inclusion of a provision on priorities, arguing that, in any event, victims with personal injuries would be taken care of under their State's social security system.

Exonerations

Following the lead of most national legislation, a draft amendment would limit the exoneration of the operator to cases in which he proves the danger was caused directly by an act of armed conflict, hostilities, civil war or insurrection. As terrorism is not specifically mentioned, the operator could be held liable for damage caused by acts of terrorism. This would depend on whether the terrorism was determined to be part of an armed conflict or civil war or simply an isolated act. In any event, operators should be able to anticipate and be prepared for deliberate acts of damage perpetrated by third parties. Finally, if the amendment is adopted, the operator would be liable for damage caused by a nuclear accident directly due to a natural disaster.

Settlement of Disputes

In place of the existing optional protocol on the settlement of disputes, which has not entered into force, it has been suggested that the revised *Vienna Convention* include a new article addressing the question of disputes concerning the interpretation or application of the Convention. In the event of a dispute the parties would be required, first, to consult with a view to settlement by negotiation or other peaceful means, and second, should the dispute not be settled within six months, to submit it either to arbitration or to the International Court of Justice.

Since many States do not wish to be legally bound to submit a dispute to arbitration or to the International Court, the Convention would provide an opting out procedure whereby a State could declare that it does not accept either means of resolving the dispute.

State Responsibility (or Liability)

Although neither the *Paris* nor the *Vienna Convention*s contain any provisions applying the principle of State responsibility or enabling State-to-State claims, both explicitly reserve the question, in the following terms:

Paris Convention, Annex II:

This convention shall not be interpreted as depriving a Contracting Party, on whose territory damage was caused by a nuclear incident occurring on the territory of another Contracting Party, of any recourse which might be available to it under international law.

Vienna Convention, Article XVIII:

This Convention shall not be construed as affecting the rights, if any, of a Contracting Party under the general rules of public international law in respect of nuclear damage.

In the context of the revision of the *Vienna Convention*, some of the countries involved in the negotiations wish to include aspects of State liability in the amendments. Essentially, these would amount to both a declaration on principle and a provision for its practical application. First, there would be an express recognition of Principle 21 of the *Stockholm Declaration on the Human Environment* in relation to nuclear activities; that is, that States have the duty to ensure that nuclear activities within their jurisdiction and control do not cause damage to the environment of other States or to areas beyond the limits of national jurisdiction.

Second, States would be required to pay compensation for any damage that remained uncompensated after the exhaustion of the operator's liability under the Convention and the application of any other agreements, such as one for supplementary funding.

In favour of such provisions, proponents point out that States are implicated in the risk created by nuclear installations, as they decide to license them in the first place and are at all times responsible for regulating them and ensuring their safe operation. Therefore, it would only be fair and equitable that the installation State bear part of the burden of the damage. Otherwise, the victims would have to bear it themselves, which appears to be manifestly unfair. Furthermore, if the installation State were liable, it might have an additional incentive to enforce the most stringent safety requirements.

However, many States oppose this proposal, for a variety of different reasons. While some believe that nothing should be done on the issue pending the outcome of the deliberations of the International Law Commission, others consider that it would be awkward or inappropriate to join the concepts of State responsibility and civil liability in the same legal instrument. For, the civil liability conventions provide for actions under private domestic law in the regular national courts, and State responsibility would entail claims between States and ultimate dispute settlement in an international forum, either by inter-State arbitration or before the International Court of Justice.

On the other hand, there appears to be general agreement that the words "if any" and "in respect of nuclear damage" should be deleted from Article XVIII. Furthermore, even if the concept of State liability is somewhat controversial, that of a supplementary State funding of compensation is generally accepted.

Chapter IX

AN INTERNATIONAL SCHEME FOR SUPPLEMENTARY FUNDING

Providing Adequate Compensation

In the wake of the accident at Three Mile Island in 1979, which caused no off-site releases of radioactivity, insurance companies, however, paid out more than 25 million dollars, mainly for the cost of evacuations. A few years later, the accident at Chernobyl caused billions of dollars worth of damage not only in the immediate vicinity, but also throughout eastern and western Europe. In the light of this experience, there is no doubt that even with a greatly increased liability limit under the revised *Vienna Convention*, the operator's financial security may not afford full compensation to the victims of even a non-catastrophic nuclear accident.

The question of finding some means to provide additional funds for compensation was therefore included in the negotiations being held under the auspices of the IAEA. At the same time as it is considering the revisions to the *Vienna Convention*, the Standing Committee on Nuclear Damage is also examining the possibility of a convention on supplementary funding, somewhat like the *Brussels Convention*, that would provide additional funds for compensation when the operator's financial security proves insufficient.

The general assumption behind the negotiations has been that the new convention on supplementary funding would be an integral component of the system established by the *Paris* and *Vienna Conventions* linked by the *Joint Protocol*. Under the supplementary funding convention, additional compensation would be made available to the victims of nuclear damage for which an operator is liable under either the *Paris* or the *Vienna Convention*, when the allowable claims exceed his liability limit, provided that the courts of a State party have jurisdiction under either of the two main conventions.

During the years that these negotiations have been going on, many different ideas and proposed schemes have been put forward. Although there is general agreement in principle that a supplementary funding scheme is desirable, at the time of writing no agreement has been reached on a precise proposal. This chapter will, therefore, analyse the issues which have been raised during the negotiations, but cannot attempt to predict the final result.

Sources of Funding

As described in Chapter IV, the *Brussels Convention* provides for three tiers of funding – the financial security of the operator (under the *Paris Convention*), public funds of the installation State, and collective contributions of public funds from all the Contracting Parties. It is generally agreed among delegations in Vienna that these sources of funding should also be used in the new global scheme.

The contribution by the installation State is seen as desirable, because that State holds the power of decision to permit a nuclear industry within its jurisdiction. It also licenses each installation, regulates its operation and is responsible both for establishing safety regulations and for enforcing them. It is believed that a requirement to contribute to compensating the victims of an accident would induce the installation State to introduce and enforce the highest possible safety standards.

Collective contributions by States parties are a mark of international solidarity, as well as increasing the amount which can be collected for the compensation of nuclear damage (like funding by the installation State).

Early in the negotiations in Vienna, however, it was proposed that the new supplementary funding mechanism should add to these sources of funding a new one – collective contributions from the nuclear industry in all the Contracting Parties. The national law of certain countries, such as the United States, Germany and Switzerland, already provides for compensation funds made up of collective contributions from nuclear operators.

Contributions from the nuclear industry could, for example, be raised by means of a compulsory levy on all operators of nuclear installations in the Contracting Parties in the case of an accident. This "levy" approach might result in funds for compensation being raised as follows:

1. up to a specified limit (probably the liability limit in the revised *Vienna Convention*) or any higher amount applicable under national law, funds from the operator's insurance or other financial security;

2. up to a second specified limit, public funds provided by the installation State, as in the *Brussels Convention*;

3. beyond the amount paid by the installation State, funds provided by contributions from the operators of nuclear installations situated in the territories of all the States parties, in accordance with a scale of contributions based upon criteria such as the thermal power of the nuclear installations involved and the particular characteristics of their inventory of radioactive material; and

4. if some of the damage still remains uncompensated, public funds to be made available by the States parties.

Some delegations in the Vienna negotiations, however, are opposed to the "levy" approach. Some oppose in principle the idea of a compulsory levy, preferring that contributions should be worked out through commercial arrangements between operators. Most opponents also point out that the national safety standards vary greatly. They consider it unjust that operators who are obliged by their national law to observe high safety standards should be forced to contribute to the payment of damages for which an operator of an "unsafe" installation in another country is liable. This, they argue, undermines incentives for States and operators to run their nuclear plants according to the highest standards, and is therefore contrary to the real interests of potential victims as well as to the principle that the "polluter pays". Some delegations putting forward this view would prefer operators to be required to contribute to compensation only if an operator with whom they have chosen to join in a "risk pool" is liable.

It has been suggested that such a scheme might be established by setting the operator's liability limit at an amount considerably higher than the minimum financial security required to be held by the operator under the *Paris* and *Vienna Conventions*. It would be up to the operator how he met this obligation. In part it would be covered, as now, by insurance. In most cases, however, private insurance would not be available to cover the total liability amount. It would be possible for the rest of the amount to be covered by a guarantee from the installation State, as is presently the case under the *Paris* and *Vienna Conventions*. However, rather than rely on a State guarantee, operators would be expected to cover part of their potential liability through membership of a risk pool. The risk pools would be organised on a commercial basis, with contracts binding the members to contribute funds to compensate the victims in the event of a nuclear accident in one of the installations covered by the pool, causing sufficient damage to bring the supplementary funding convention into play.

137

Beyond the amount of the operator's liability, public funds would be made available by the installation State, and then by collective contributions of public funds by the States parties.

Since the members of each risk pool would join together voluntarily, certain operators might be unable to join any pool because of a perception that their safety standards were inadequate. In these cases, the installation State would have to guarantee the required amounts of compensation, and thus bear a greater financial burden in the case of an accident than those States whose operators participated in pools. While some regard this as an advantage, as it gives States an incentive to raise safety standards, others fear that such a scheme will simply deter the countries whose operators may not be able to join a pool from ratifying the Convention.

Since the countries in question are precisely those in which the risks of an accident are greatest, their exclusion from the supplementary funding system would be regrettable. This is indeed one of the basic problems which has arisen in the negotiations. On the one hand, the international community wishes those States in which nuclear accidents are most likely to happen to be covered by the nuclear liability regime. On the other, there are doubts as to the possibility of effectively providing insurance for the nuclear installations concerned, and so possibly encouraging States to keep open nuclear power plants which, for safety reasons, should be closed down. The "optional risk pool" approach is one suggestion for dealing with this problem. Another is to provide for an option to exclude certain nuclear installations from the supplementary funding scheme. This possibility is dealt with below.

Although the idea of collective contributions from industry has been welcomed in theory, it has not, after several years of negotiations, proved possible to agree even on the broad basis on which those contributions would be made – whether through fixed levy or optional pool. It may be, therefore, that this source of funding will not in the end be included in the Convention, and that the new supplementary funding mechanism, like the *Brussels Convention*, will rely solely on public funds.

Calculation of Contributions

The calculation of the contributions of the liable operator and of the installation State, under the supplementary funding Convention, can be expected to be relatively simple. The amount of the contribution by the liable operator will be fixed by national legislation, in accordance with a set minimum amount. The amount of the installation State contribution will depend on the level of the operator's liability, since the State will have to pay in funds beyond that level up to a set amount.

In relation to collective contributions, whether by industry or the States parties, however, formulae will have to be worked out.

Two basic approaches are possible. According to the first – that in the *Brussels Convention* – an overall amount is set, and each contributor must pay a percentage of that total amount, according to the formula for contributions. Thus the total compensation available does not vary, but the greater the number of parties/operators, the lower the individual contributions. The second approach would be based on fixed contributions, according to a formula, for each party/operator. This would result in a total amount of compensation which would vary according to the number of parties to the Convention and the number of operators in each of them, as well as according to any variables in the formula for contributions.

The contribution by each nuclear operator would most likely depend, in general terms, on the extent of the risk created by that operator's installations. The formula for contributions would therefore be based on the type and size of installation, using factors such as thermal power and the inventory of radioactive material in the installation. It is possible that certain installations – such as small research reactors – might be exempted from contributions, if they create no risk of off-site damage.

A similar criterion could be used – at least in part – to calculate the contribution of each Contracting Party to the collective State funding in the final tier of compensation. That is to say, a certain percentage of each Contracting Party's contribution would be based on the ratio between the thermal power (or risk factor calculated in some other way) of nuclear installations in that country, and the total thermal power in all Contracting Parties.

Other elements might also be taken into account in calculating each Contracting Party's contribution. On the model of the *Brussels Convention*, for example, a percentage of the contribution could be based on the relative wealth of the country concerned, as indicated by gross national product, or the scale of assessments for contributions to the United Nations. Other possible elements are nuclear power consumption, consumption of electricity in general, income from uranium mining etc.

If factors other than the risk associated with each country's nuclear installations are taken into account, countries which do not have nuclear installations may be required to contribute to supplementary funding. Under the

Brussels Convention, they do so. It has been argued that this is reasonable, because the supplementary funding scheme is analogous to a form of insurance, or simply as an indication of international solidarity. Another argument which has been put forward is that all countries in fact benefit from nuclear power, whether or not they have nuclear power programmes, either directly through the importation of nuclear-generated electricity or indirectly because the use of nuclear power reduces global pollution from the burning of fossil fuels. However, many "non-nuclear" States argue that since they do not contribute to the risk with which the Convention deals, they should not have to contribute funds.

In fact, few countries have no nuclear installations at all within their territory, since even small research reactors fall within the definition of "nuclear installation" in the *Paris* and *Vienna Conventions*. A subsidiary question therefore is whether such small installations – which it is hard to imagine causing transboundary damage – should be taken into account in deciding whether, and to what extent, a Contracting Party is to contribute to the fund.

It has also been suggested that there be a maximum which might be charged to any operator or Contracting Party.

Installation State Funding: A Proposal for State Funding in *the* Vienna Convention

As already mentioned, it appears to be generally accepted that the installation State should be required to make a contribution, beyond that of other States parties, when an accident occurs in an installation subject to its regulatory control. This contribution may be reduced proportionally if the installation State imposes a high liability limit on its operator. This approach is taken in the *Brussels Convention*, and has been part of most schemes proposed for the new supplementary funding Convention.

Another proposal, however, would include an obligation for the installation State to provide funds in the basic – Paris or Vienna – Convention. In this way an element of supplementary funding would be provided by the basic Convention, without the need for the State concerned to be a party to a supplementary funding Convention.

To achieve this, the *Paris* or *Vienna Convention* could require the installation State to ensure that funds are paid up to a given amount by either:

a) setting the operator's liability at that figure, and providing a financial guarantee to the operator for any part of the amount which could not be covered by insurance or another type of guarantee; or

b) setting the operator's liability limit at a lower figure, and undertaking to contribute the rest itself.

These options are analogous to provisions of the *Brussels Convention*, which were intended to meet the requirements of different national legal systems.

If this approach is followed, the question arises whether the funds made available by the State must be payable to compensate exactly the same damage, and under the same conditions, as funds payable by the operator. It would be possible to provide, for example, that the funds payable by the operator should be used to compensate damage in non-contracting States, but that the extra public funds paid by the State, should not. Equally, it would be possible to impose a requirement of reciprocity in relation to an extra installation State tier of funding. That is to say that the extra funds from the installation State would be payable only for damage suffered in a State which, in the case of an accident in its territory, would provide funds up to the same level.

If installation State funding is included in the basic convention, it might not be thought necessary or desirable to provide for an installation State contribution also in the supplementary funding convention.

Scope

The new supplementary funding Convention is intended to provide additional funding once the compensation available from the liable operator's financial security is exhausted, and therefore would apply only where an operator of a nuclear installation situated in the territory of a Contracting Party to that Convention is liable.

However, an important question to be decided is the geographical scope of its application; that is to say where nuclear damage must be suffered in order to qualify for supplementary compensation. The normal rule is that an international agreement benefits only those States which are parties to it. The *Brussels Convention* follows this approach, in that it provides compensation only for damage suffered in the territory of a Contracting Party, or, in the case of damage on the high seas, by a national, or on a ship or aircraft operated by a Contracting Party. It is possible that a similar approach will be followed in the new supplementary funding Convention.

However, as mentioned in Chapter VIII, it has been proposed that the revised *Vienna Convention* itself should apply to damage suffered in States which are not parties. It is not necessary that the scope of the supplementary funding Convention should follow exactly the same principle as the basic Convention. Since the contribution of public funds by the States parties is involved, certain delegations think it reasonable that supplementary funding should be payable only for damage suffered in those States which have undertaken the obligations in the new Convention. Others, however, would be in favour of paying compensation for damage in non-contracting States which do not have nuclear installations.

Transboundary Damage

The *Brussels Convention* applies to damage within the territory of the installation State as well as that suffered in other States, and discussions on supplementary funding have so far generally assumed this would also be the case for the new Convention. However, it has been suggested that supplementary funds should be available exclusively for transboundary damage, i.e., that suffered in States other than the installation State.

Exclusion of Certain Installations

As already mentioned, there is concern in some quarters that public funds should not be used, through this Convention, as a form of subsidy for States which have nuclear installations with inadequate safety standards. A proposal has been made that a party to the supplementary funding Convention should be permitted to declare that it would not provide funding for damage caused by particular foreign nuclear installation. If a nuclear accident occurred in the installation concerned, then the party which had made the declaration would not be obliged to contribute funds. Neither, however, would supplementary compensation be made available for nuclear damage suffered in the territory of the declaring State as a result of that accident.

The right to make such a declaration could be made subject to conditions. In particular it has been suggested that a declaration could not be made in relation to an installation under the authority of a State that had adhered to an international agreement on assuring agreed nuclear safety standards. The instrument envisaged was the *Nuclear Safety Convention* mentioned in Chapter VI, which at the time of the proposal was still being negotiated under the auspices of the IAEA. Since the Convention as finally adopted provides for undertakings which are very general in nature, and the only enforcement mechanism is that of peer review, it may be that adherence to it will now not be regarded as sufficient grounds to forbid a declaration of exclusion. If the *Safety Convention* exception is retained, however, the proposal as a whole can be regarded as an inducement to States to join that Convention.

However, the whole idea of optional exclusion is very controversial. Some States argue that it is inappropriate to introduce notions of enforcement of safety standards into a liability convention, and many consider political implications and potential practical consequences to be unacceptable. It is far from certain that this proposal will be adopted.

Parties to a Supplementary Funding Convention

The original conception of the supplementary funding Convention was that it would complement both the Paris and *Vienna Conventions*. Some doubts have, however, been raised in this regard.

In the first place, it is likely that at least for a transition period, there will be in existence a revised *Vienna Convention* and an unrevised *Vienna Convention*, and eventually a revised and an unrevised *Paris Convention*, and in addition the *Joint Protocol* which links the *Paris* and *Vienna Conventions* "and any amendment thereto which is in force for a Contracting Party [to the *Joint Protocol*]". It is necessary to decide whether the supplementary funding Convention is to be open to Parties to all of these instruments, or only to some. The approach which would ensure the greatest uniformity would be to require a State to be a Party to either the revised *Vienna Convention* or a revised *Paris Convention* as well as the *Joint Protocol*. This might, however, limit the number of Parties. Greater coverage would be ensured by allowing Parties to any of the existing Conventions, in their amended or unamended form, to join the new supplementary funding Convention, but in that case that Convention will have to take into account widely varying national legal regimes.

Indeed, the very requirement that parties to the new supplementary funding Convention should be members of the Paris/Vienna regime has been challenged. There has been a proposal that a State should be entitled to join a supplementary funding scheme whether or not it is a party to the *Vienna* or *Paris Convention*, provided its national legal regime includes certain of the basic principles in those Conventions, and subject to a given threshold for the operator's liability limit.

Regional Agreements

The discussions in Vienna have assumed that the new supplementary funding Convention would aim at universal participation. Some delegations however, have suggested that the economic differences – as well as differences in safety standards – between various countries make this aim is impracticable, and that a regional approach would be preferable. They also point out that in the case of an accident nuclear damage is much more likely to be suffered in nearby States. Regional agreements could replace, or complement, a global supplementary funding convention. Indeed, the supplementary funding Convention is likely to include a provision preserving the right of any party to conclude a special agreement concerning compensation for nuclear damage with a country that is not a party, provided that such an agreement does not create any additional obligations for other parties. There is a similar provision in the *Brussels Convention*, which has permitted Germany to conclude a convention on compensation for nuclear damage with Switzerland.

Current Status of the Negotiations

Many decisions, therefore, remain to be made concerning fundamental aspects of the new supplementary funding scheme. Some States have indeed proposed setting the supplementary funding convention aside temporarily to concentrate on reaching agreement on the Vienna revision as soon as possible. However, others insist upon negotiating both conventions at the same time, considering that the revised *Vienna Convention* alone would not afford sufficient protection to the victims. The current approach is to proceed with both the Vienna revision and the supplementary funding convention simultaneously.

Chapter X

TENTATIVE CONCLUSIONS

The States involved in the nuclear field in the late 1950s responded to the economic exigencies of developing an entirely new form of energy by establishing a legal framework that was remarkably advanced for its time and that was in many ways surprisingly prescient. Not only the legislators, but also the insurers managed, at a time when very little was known about the deleterious consequences of nuclear accidents, to constitute a liability regime that, for 20-25 years, met the needs for protection of potential victims of nuclear damage until two accidents, one minor and the other major, revealed certain deficiencies, some already understood, but others which could not have been predicted.

Even before Chernobyl, it was known that the liability limits in the international conventions were too low; however, the damage that was caused was far greater than anyone had anticipated. Not only were the physical and economic consequences devastating near the site of the accident, but also the radioactive fallout covered a more extensive area than anyone had imagined, and some types of damage were almost entirely unexpected. No one had suspected that areas thousands of miles away would be affected; no one had expected the extent of damage to the environment or the heavy losses suffered by farmers and those in related occupations in countries as distant as the Nordic countries, Germany or the United Kingdom. No one had thought either of the disruptions in international trade caused by contaminated products, or the possibilities of pure economic loss, such as a decrease in tourism.

When the ramifications of the accident at Chernobyl were understood, the international community moved to fill the gaps in the regime. Nationally, some States revised their liability legislation, in particular, to raise the amounts of compensation. Others engaged in a more fundamental reconsideration of the nuclear option, while all enhanced their nuclear safety programmes. Internationally, States collectively embarked upon negotiations to develop new conventions at the same time as revising the old. New conventions were concluded in relation to emergency response concerning the early notification of an accident and international assistance to the victims, and in relation to liability, in the *Joint Protocol* to link the *Paris* and *Vienna Conventions*.

Yet, the *Joint Protocol* was just a stop-gap measure, and a more extensive reconsideration of the international liability regime was necessary. Following an initial flurry of interest in State liability, a decision was taken to revise the *Vienna Convention* and to devise a mechanism for supplementary funding where operator liability was insufficient to compensate all the victims. However, the revision of the *Vienna Convention* and a possible new convention on additional funding cannot stand alone, as there will inevitably be repercussions on the *Paris* and *Brussels Conventions*.

The *Vienna Convention(s)*

Negotiations regarding the revision of the *Vienna Convention* are proceeding very slowly, much more slowly than had initially been expected. Since 1989, scores of proposals have been advanced and discussed. Gradually, those with little or no support have been discarded, with a hard core remaining, all of which enjoy a substantial degree of support among a considerable number of States. However, no proposals have yet been definitively adopted.

Of those discussed in Chapter VIII, some have encountered no opposition and will almost certainly be adopted. An example is the change in the unit of account to the SDR. On the other hand, other proposals are so controversial or have encountered so much opposition that it is difficult to imagine an early compromise, or even any compromise at all. As for State liability, the subject is so sensitive, that until now (October 1994) it has scarcely been broached. Finally, although there is general agreement that the liability levels must be increased, there has yet to be a focussed discussion of what the new amounts should be.

To a certain extent, the latter issue is linked to the development of the convention on supplementary funding. The negotiations on this convention are part of the reason for the delay, as agreement on a suitable mechanism for supplementary funding may be even more distant than that on the revision of the *Vienna Convention*. For some time, there has been disagreement as to whether the two conventions should be developed in parallel or whether in order to save time, the *Vienna Convention* should be concluded first, before a concerted effort is made on supplementary funding.

At present, negotiations on both are proceeding simultaneously, as many States believe that the protection provided by the *Vienna Convention* would be so insufficient without the additional compensation, that the *Vienna Convention* would not be worth adopting on its own. For the moment, therefore, the two conventions are tied together, stumbling forward with some difficulty. It was this same insufficiency of the *Vienna Convention* alone that prompted the new proposal to include funding by the installation State in the "main convention". As this idea is still under consideration, it is not impossible that a compromise may be found.

Consequently, the reader must bear in mind that the description of the negotiations in Chapters VIII and IX is a description of proposals only. The final text of the conventions may differ, perhaps considerably, from the current proposals, and agreement may be only be reached several years in the future.

The *Paris* and *Brussels Conventions*

After the revision of the *Vienna Convention*, the next challenge for the international community will be the revision of the *Paris* and perhaps the *Brussels Conventions*. Due to the existence of the NEA Group of Governmental Experts, the *Paris* and *Brussels Conventions* are subject to a process of continuous review. At its twice yearly meetings, the group is always seeking ways to improve the Conventions by means of decisions and recommendations, if not by formal amendments. After Chernobyl, the group of course realised that "its" conventions had to be revised, for many of the same reasons that provoked the revision of the *Vienna Convention*. For example, liability limits had to be raised, the expansion of the definition of damage had to be considered, and so forth.

From September 1986 to September 1988, the NEA was involved in the negotiation of the *Joint Protocol*, along with the IAEA. Then, when the discussions on the revision of the liability regime commenced in Vienna, any consideration of the revision of the *Paris Convention* was suspended, pending the outcome of the negotiations at the IAEA. Since that time the group has been preoccupied largely with working out common positions with respect to the revision of the nuclear liability regime and the creation of a new convention on supplementary funding.

For, the *Paris Convention* will have to be revised, not only because it requires improvement for its own sake, but also because it is linked to the *Vienna Convention* by the *Joint Protocol*. As a consequence, the parties to the *Paris Convention* are anxious to see the *Vienna Convention* revised in a manner that corresponds to what they desire in the *Paris Convention*. Obviously, in order for the *Joint Protocol* system to be effective, the two Conventions must be harmonized. If the proposals to amend the *Vienna Convention* are adopted, the existing differences between the two Conventions will only increase, thus possibly compromising the operation of the *Joint Protocol*.

Yet, it is not only the *Paris Convention* that will be affected by the implementation of the *Joint Protocol* and by the negotiations in Vienna. First, the *Joint Protocol* will extend the operation of the *Paris Convention* to non-parties, thereby increasing the number of potential victims and causing the State funding mechanism of the *Brussels Convention* to come into effect much earlier than otherwise. Under the terms of the *Brussels Convention*, States parties must expressly consent its application in such a situation. They have agreed to do so.

Furthermore, in November 1992, the OECD Council recommended that States parties take appropriate measures to ensure that operators or carriers under their jurisdiction assume liability in all cases of transport between such installations and installations in *Vienna Convention* States also party to the *Joint Protocol*. Thus, the application of the *Brussels Convention* will be preserved in transport cases where the *Joint Protocol* might exclude its application.

Finally, the adoption of a convention on supplementary funding will have inevitable consequences for the fate of the *Brussels Convention*, as whatever proposal is finally adopted, it will be necessary to consider whether it should exist in parallel with, or supersede, the *Brussels Convention*. Therefore, it is possible that the *Brussels Convention* may become defunct. However, if States cannot agree on a new convention on supplementary funding, then the *Brussels Convention* may continue, albeit in a slightly amended form.

A third possibility is that States may decide to implement the suggestion that regional conventions on supplementary funding may be more appropriate and more acceptable than a global one.

Radioactive Waste

More doubtful still, because in an earlier stage of development, is the future of any proposals regarding liability for damage caused by the disposal of radioactive waste. The question of liability for damage in the pre-closure phase of a nuclear waste facility has been resolved under the *Paris Convention*, and has now been raised but not discussed in the context of the *Vienna Convention*. Moreover, although the consideration of liability during the post-closure phase has been initiated in the NEA Group of Governmental Experts, discussions are likely to continue for some years.

Conclusions

Time and unfortunate experience have shown that the international regime relating to liability for nuclear damage is in need of considerable improvement. This is hardly surprising, as the international conventions were developed when the nuclear industry was in its infancy and its implications were not fully understood. However, States are now actively engaged in the process of modernising and expanding the liability system to overcome the existing problems. Due to the varied interests and attitudes of the States involved, the process may continue for some years.

In this publication the liability regime as it now stands, as well as some of the proposals for its improvement have been described. Only time will tell how the challenges for the future will ultimately be met.

SELECTIVE BIBLIOGRAPHY

OECD/NEA Publications

Third Party Liability and Insurance in the Field of Maritime Carriage of Nuclear Substances, Monaco Symposium, International Atomic Energy Agency and OECD European Nuclear Energy Agency, OECD, *Paris*, 1968.

Long-Term Management of Radioactive Waste: Legal, Administrative and Financial Aspects, OECD/NEA, *Paris*, 1984.

Nuclear Third Party Liability and Insurance: Status and Prospects, Munich Symposium, OECD Nuclear Energy Agency and International Atomic Energy Agency, OECD, Paris, 1985.

Nuclear Accidents: Intervention Levels for the Protection of the Population, OECD Nuclear Energy Agency, Paris, 1989.

Paris Convention on Third Party Liability in the Field of Nuclear Energy and *Brussels Convention Supplementary to the Paris Convention*, OECD Nuclear Energy Agency, Paris, 1989.

Third Party Liability, OECD Nuclear Energy Agency, Paris, 1990.

Protection of the Population in the Event of a Nuclear Accident: A Basis for Intervention, OECD Nuclear Energy Agency, Paris, 1990.

Paris Convention: Decisions, Recommendations, Interpretations, OECD Nuclear Energy Agency, Paris, 1990.

Nuclear Accidents: Liabilities and Guarantees, Helsinki Symposium, OECD Nuclear Energy Agency and International Atomic Energy Agency, OECD, Paris, 1993.

IAEA Publications

Civil Liability for Nuclear Damage: *Official Records*, International Conference, Vienna, 29 April-19 May 1963, IAEA Legal Series No. 2, International Atomic Energy Agency, Vienna, 1964.

International Conventions on Civil Liability for Nuclear Damage, IAEA Legal Series No. 4, Vienna, 1976.

Convention on Early Notification of a Nuclear Accident and Convention on Assistance in the Case of a Nuclear Accident or Radiological Emergency, IAEA Legal Series No. 14, Vienna, 1987.

Nuclear Liability: Joint Protocol Relating to the Application of the Vienna Convention and the Paris Convention, 1988; Final Act of the Conference on the Relationship between the *Paris Convention* and the *Vienna Convention*, Vienna, 21 September 1988, and Text of the *Joint Protocol*, International Atomic Energy Agency, Vienna, 1989.

Books

Dow, J. *Nuclear Energy and Insurance,* Whiter by and Co, London, 1989.

Cameron, P., Hancher, L., and Kühn, W., ed., *Nuclear Energy Law after Chernobyl*, Graham & Trotman, London/Dordrecht/Boston and International Bar Association, 1988.

Lopuski, Jan, *Liability for Nuclear Damage: An International Perspective – Reflections on the Revision of the* Vienna Convention, National Atomic Energy Agency, Warsaw, 1993.

Articles

The Nuclear Law Bulletin (NLB), published twice yearly by the NEA, frequently contains legislation, reports and articles on nuclear liability issues. See also articles in the *NEA Newsletter*:

- Moser, B., "Proof of Damage from Ionizing Radiation", NLB, No. 38.
- Pelzer, N., "Current Problems of Nuclear Liability Law in the Post-Chernobyl Period", NLB, No. 39.

– Holtz, C., "The Concept of Property Damage and Related Issues in Liability Law – Possible Implications for the *Paris Convention on Third Party Liability in the Field of Nuclear Energy*", NLB, No. 40.

– Rowden, M.A., J. R. Kramer and L.M. Cuoco, "The Price-Anderson Amendments Act of 1988: A Case of Better Late Than Never", NLB, No. 42.

– von Büsekist, O., "A Bridge Between Two Conventions on Civil Liability for Nuclear Damage: the Joint Protocol Relating to the Application of the *Vienna Convention* and the *Paris Convention*", NLB, No. 43.

– La Fayette, L. de, "Towards a New Régime of State Responsibility for Nuclear Activities", NLB, No. 50.

– La Fayette, L. de, "Nuclear Liability Revisited", 1 Review of European Community and International Environmental Law 443.

– Strohl, P., "La *Convention de 1971 relative à la responsabilité civile dans le domaine du transport maritime de matières nucléaires*", in *Annuaire français de droit international*, CNRS, Paris, 1972.

– Reyners, P., "Limiting the Liability of the Nuclear Operator", *NEA Newsletter*, 1986.

SCHEDULES

PARIS CONVENTION ON THIRD PARTY LIABILITY IN THE FIELD OF NUCLEAR ENERGY OF 29 JULY 1960, AS AMENDED BY THE *ADDITIONAL PROTOCOL OF 28 JANUARY 1964* AND BY THE *PROTOCOL OF 16 NOVEMBER 1982*

The GOVERNMENTS of the Federal Republic of Germany, the Republic of Austria, the Kingdom of Belgium, the Kingdom of Denmark, the Kingdom of Spain, the Republic of Finland, the French Republic, the Hellenic Republic, the Italian Republic, the Grand Duchy of Luxembourg, the Kingdom of Norway, the Kingdom of the Netherlands, the Portuguese Republic, the United Kingdom of Great Britain and Northern Ireland, the Kingdom of Sweden, the Swiss Confederation and the Turkish Republic,

CONSIDERING that the OECD Nuclear Energy Agency, established within the framework of the Organisation for Economic Co-operation and Development (hereinafter referred to as the "Organisation"), is charged with encouraging the elaboration and harmonization of legislation relating to nuclear energy in participating countries, in particular with regard to third party liability and insurance against atomic risks;

DESIROUS of ensuring adequate and equitable compensation for persons who suffer damage caused by nuclear incidents whilst taking the necessary steps to ensure that the development of the production and uses of nuclear energy for peaceful purposes is not thereby hindered;

CONVINCED of the need for unifying the basic rules applying in the various countries to the liability incurred for such damage, whilst leaving these countries free to take, on a national basis, any additional measures which they deem appropriate;

HAVE AGREED as follows:

Article 1

a)   For the purposes of this Convention:

i)   "a nuclear incident" means any occurrence or succession of occurrences having the same origin which causes damage, provided that such occurrence or succession of occurrences, or any of the damage caused, arises out of or results either from the radioactive properties, or a combination of radioactive properties with toxic, explosive, or other hazardous properties of nuclear fuel or radioactive products or waste or with any of them, or from ionising radiations emitted by any source of radiation inside a nuclear installation;

ii)   "nuclear installation" means reactors other than those comprised in any means of transport; factories for the manufacture or processing of nuclear substances; factories for the separation of isotopes of nuclear fuel; factories for the reprocessing of irradiated nuclear fuel; facilities for the storage of nuclear substances other than storage incidental to the carriage of such substances; and such other installations in which there are nuclear fuel or radioactive products or waste as the Steering Committee for Nuclear Energy of the Organisation (hereinafter referred to as the "Steering Committee") shall from time to time determine; any Contracting Party may determine that two or more nuclear installations of one operator which are located on the same site shall, together with any other premises on that site where radioactive material is held, be treated as a single nuclear installation;

iii)   "nuclear fuel" means fissionable material in the form of uranium metal, alloy, or chemical compound (including natural uranium), plutonium metal, alloy, or chemical compound, and such other fissionable material as the Steering Committee shall from time to time determine;

iv)   "radioactive products or waste" means any radioactive material produced in or made radioactive by exposure to the radiation incidental to the process of producing or utilising nuclear fuel, but does not include (1) nuclear fuel, or (2) radioisotopes outside a nuclear installation which have reached the final stage of fabrication so as to be usable for any industrial, commercial, agricultural, medical, scientific or educational purpose;

v)   "nuclear substances" means nuclear fuel (other than natural uranium and other than depleted uranium) and radioactive products or waste.

vi) "Operator" in relation to a nuclear installation means the person designated or recognised by the competent public authority as the operator of that installation.

b) The Steering Committee may, if in its view the small extent of the risks involved so warrants, exclude any nuclear installation, nuclear fuel, or nuclear substances from the application of this Convention.

Article 2

This Convention does not apply to nuclear incidents occurring in the territory of non-Contracting States or to damage suffered in such territory, unless otherwise provided by the legislation of the Contracting Party in whose territory the nuclear installation of the operator liable is situated, and except in regard to rights referred to in Article 6(e).

Article 3

a) The operator of a nuclear installation shall be liable, in accordance with this Convention, for:

i) damage to or loss of life of any person; and

ii) damage to or loss of any property other than:

1. the nuclear installation itself and any other nuclear installation, including a nuclear installation under construction, on the site where that installation is located; and

2. any property on that same site which is used or to be used in connection with any such installation, upon proof that such damage or loss (hereinafter referred to as "damage") was caused by a nuclear incident in such installation or involving nuclear substances coming from such installation, except as otherwise provided for in Article 4.

b) Where the damage or loss is caused jointly by a nuclear incident and by an incident other than a nuclear incident, that part of the damage or loss which is caused by such other incident, shall, to the extent that it is not reasonably separable from the damage or loss caused by the nuclear incident, be considered to be damage caused by the nuclear incident. Where the damage or loss is caused jointly by a nuclear incident and by an emission of ionising radiation not covered by this Convention, nothing in this Convention shall limit or otherwise affect the liability of any person in connection with that emission of ionising radiation.

156

Article 4

In the case of carriage of nuclear substances, including storage incidental thereto, without prejudice to Article 2:

a) the operator of a nuclear installation shall be liable, in accordance with this Convention, for damage upon proof that it was caused by a nuclear incident outside that installation and involving nuclear substances in the course of carriage therefrom, only if the incident occurs:

    i) before liability with regard to nuclear incidents involving the nuclear substances has been assumed, pursuant to the express terms of a contract in writing, by the operator of another nuclear installation;

    ii) in the absence of such express terms, before the operator of another nuclear installation has taken charge of the nuclear substances; or

    iii) where the nuclear substances are intended to be used in a reactor comprised in a means of transport, before the person duly authorized to operate that reactor has taken charge of the nuclear substances; but

    iv) where the nuclear substances have been sent to a person within the territory of a non-Contracting State, before they have been unloaded from the means of transport by which they have arrived in the territory of that non-Contracting State.

b) the operator of a nuclear installation shall be liable, in accordance with this Convention, for damage upon proof that it was caused by a nuclear incident outside that installation and involving nuclear substances in the course of carriage thereto, only if the incident occurs:

    i) after liability with regard to nuclear incidents involving the nuclear substances has been assumed by him, pursuant to the express terms of a contract in writing, from the operator of another nuclear installation;

    ii) in the absence of such express terms, after he has taken charge of the nuclear substances; or

    iii) after he has taken charge of the nuclear substances from a person operating a reactor comprised in a means of transport; but

    iv) where the nuclear substances have, with the written consent of the operator, been sent from a person within the territory of a non-Contracting State, after they have been loaded on the means of transport by which they are to be carried from the territory of that State.

c)   the operator liable in accordance with this Convention shall provide the carrier with a certificate issued by or on behalf of the insurer or other financial guarantor furnishing the security required pursuant to Article 10. However, a Contracting Party may exclude this obligation in relation to carriage which takes place wholly within its own territory. The certificate shall state the name and address of that operator and the amount, type and duration of the security, and these statements may not be disputed by the person by whom or on whose behalf the certificate was issued. The certificate shall also indicate the nuclear substances and the carriage in respect of which the security applies and shall include a statement by the competent public authority that the person named is an operator within the meaning of this Convention.

d)   a Contracting Party may provide by legislation that, under such terms as may be contained therein and upon fulfilment of the requirements of Article 10(a), a carrier may, at his request and with the consent of an operator of a nuclear installation situated in its territory, by decision of the competent public authority, be liable in accordance with this Convention in place of that operator. In such case for all the purposes of this Convention the carrier shall be considered, in respect of nuclear incidents occurring in the course of carriage of nuclear substances, as an operator of a nuclear installation on the territory of the Contracting Party whose legislation so provides.

Article 5

a)   If the nuclear fuel or radioactive products or waste involved in a nuclear incident have been in more than one nuclear installation and are in a nuclear installation at the time damage is caused, no operator of any nuclear installation in which they have previously been shall be liable for the damage.

b)   Where, however, damage is caused by a nuclear incident occurring in a nuclear installation and involving only nuclear substances stored therein incidentally to their carriage, the operator of the nuclear installation shall not be liable where another operator or person is liable pursuant to Article 4.

c)   If the nuclear fuel or radioactive products or waste involved in a nuclear incident have been in more than one nuclear installation and are not in a nuclear installation at the time damage is caused, no operator other than the operator of the last nuclear installation in which they were before the damage was caused or an operator who has subsequently taken them in charge, or has assumed liability therefor pursuant to the express terms of a contract in writing shall be liable for the damage.

d) If damage gives rise to liability of more than one operator in accordance with this Convention, the liability of these operators shall be joint and several: provided that where such liability arises as a result of damage caused by a nuclear incident involving nuclear substances in the course of carriage in one and the same means of transport, or, in the case of storage incidental to the carriage, in one and the same nuclear installation, the maximum total amount for which such operators shall be liable shall be the highest amount established with respect to any of them pursuant to Article 7 and provided that in no case shall any one operator be required, in respect of a nuclear incident, to pay more than the amount established with respect to him pursuant to Article 7.

Article 6

a) The right to compensation for damage caused by a nuclear incident may be exercised only against an operator liable for the damage in accordance with this Convention, or, if a direct right of action against the insurer or other financial guarantor furnishing the security required pursuant to Article 10 is given by national law, against the insurer or other financial guarantor.

b) Except as otherwise provided in this Article, no other person shall be liable for damage caused by a nuclear incident, but this provision shall not affect the application of any international agreement in the field of transport in force or open for signature, ratification or accession at the date of this Convention.

c) i) Nothing in this Convention shall affect the liability:

1. of any individual for damage caused by a nuclear incident for which the operator, by virtue of Articles 3(a)(ii)(1) and (2) or Article 9, is not liable under this Convention and which results from an act or omission of that individual done with intent to cause damage;

2. of a person duly authorized to operate a reactor comprised in a means of transport for damage caused by a nuclear incident when an operator is not liable for such damage pursuant to Articles 4(a)(iii) or (b)(iii).

ii) the operator shall incur no liability outside this Convention for damage caused by a nuclear incident.

d) Any person who has paid compensation in respect of damage caused by a nuclear incident under any international agreement referred to in paragraph (b) of this Article or under any legislation of a non-Contracting

159

State shall, up to the amount which he has paid, acquire by subrogation the rights under this Convention of the person suffering damage whom he has so compensated.

e) Any person who has his principal place of business in the territory of a Contracting Party or who is the servant of such a person and who has paid compensation in respect of damage caused by a nuclear incident occurring in the territory of a non-Contracting State or in respect of damage suffered in such territory shall, up to the amount which he has paid, acquire the rights which the person so compensated would have had against the operator but for the provisions of Article 2.

f) The operator shall have a right of recourse only:

   i) if the damage caused by a nuclear incident results from an act or omission done with intent to cause damage, against the individual acting or omitting to act with such intent;

   ii) if and to the extent that it is so provided expressly by contract.

g) If the operator has a right of recourse to any extent pursuant to paragraph (f) of this Article against any person, that person shall not, to that extent, have a right against the operator under paragraphs (d) or (e) of this Article.

h) Where provisions of national or public health insurance, social security, workmen's compensation or occupational disease compensation systems include compensation for damage caused by a nuclear incident, rights of beneficiaries of such systems and rights of recourse by virtue of such systems shall be determined by the law of the Contracting Party or by the regulations of the inter-Governmental organisation which has established such systems.

Article 7

a) The aggregate of compensation required to be paid in respect of damage caused by a nuclear incident shall not exceed the maximum liability established in accordance with this Article.

b) The maximum liability of the operator in respect of damage caused by a nuclear incident shall be 15 000 000 Special Drawing Rights as defined by the International Monetary Fund and used by it for its own operations and transactions (hereinafter referred to as "Special Drawing Rights"). However,

   i) any Contracting Party, taking into account the possibilities for the operator of obtaining the insurance or other financial security required

160

pursuant to Article 10, may establish by legislation a greater or lesser amount;

    ii) any Contracting Party, having regard to the nature of the nuclear installation or the nuclear substances involved and to the likely consequences of an incident originating therefrom, may establish a lower amount,

provided that in no event shall any amounts so established be less than 5 000 000 Special Drawing Rights. The sums mentioned above may be converted into national currency in round figures.

c) Compensation for damage caused to the means of transport on which the nuclear substances involved were at the time of the nuclear incident shall not have the effect of reducing the liability of the operator in respect of other damage to an amount less than either 5 000 000 Special Drawing Rights, or any higher amount established by the legislation of a Contracting Party.

d) The amount of liability of operators of nuclear installations in the territory of a Contracting Party established in accordance with paragraph (b) of this Article as well as the provisions of any legislation of a Contracting Party pursuant to paragraph (c) of this Article shall apply to the liability of such operators wherever the nuclear incident occurs.

e) A Contracting Party may subject the transit of nuclear substances through its territory to the condition that the maximum amount of liability of the foreign operator concerned be increased, if it considers that such amount does not adequately cover the risks of a nuclear incident in the course of the transit: provided that the maximum amount thus increased shall not exceed the maximum amount of liability of operators of nuclear installations situated in its territory.

f) The provisions of paragraph (e) of this Article shall not apply:

    i) to carriage by sea where, under international law, there is a right of entry in cases of urgent distress into the ports of such Contracting Party or a right of innocent passage through its territory; or

    ii) to carriage by air where, by agreement or under international law, there is a right to fly over or land on the territory of such Contracting Party.

g) Any interest and costs awarded by a court in actions for compensation under this Convention shall not be considered to be compensation for the purposes of this Convention and shall be payable by the operator in addition to any sum for which he is liable in accordance with this Article.

Article 8

a) the right of compensation under this Convention shall be extinguished if an action is not brought within ten years from the date of the nuclear incident. National legislation may, however, establish a period longer than ten years if measures have been taken by the Contracting Party in whose territory the nuclear installation of the operator liable is situated to cover the liability of that operator in respect of any actions for compensation begun after the expiry of the period of ten years and during such longer period: provided that such extension of the extinction period shall in no case affect the right of compensation under this Convention of any person who has brought an action in respect of loss of life or personal injury against the operator before the expiry of the period of ten years.

b) in the case of damage caused by a nuclear incident involving nuclear fuel or radioactive products or waste which, at the time of the incident have been stolen, lost, jettisoned or abandoned and have not yet been recovered, the period established pursuant to paragraph (a) of this Article shall be computed from the date of that nuclear incident, but the period shall in no case exceed twenty years from the date of the theft, loss, jettison or abandonment.

c) national legislation may establish a period of not less than two years for the extinction of the right or as a period of limitation either from the date at which the person suffering damage has knowledge or from the date at which he ought reasonably to have known of both the damage and the operator liable: provided that the period established pursuant to paragraphs (a) and (b) of this Article shall not be exceeded.

d) Where the provisions of Article 13(c)(ii) are applicable, the right of compensation shall not, however, be extinguished if, within the time provided for in paragraphs (a), (b) and (c) of this Article,

i) prior to the determination by the Tribunal referred to in Article 17, an action has been brought before any of the courts from which the Tribunal can choose; if the Tribunal determines that the competent court is a court other than that before which such action has already been brought, it may fix a date by which such action has to be brought before the competent court so determined; or

ii) a request has been made to a Contracting Party concerned to initiate a determination by the Tribunal of the competent court pursuant to Article 13(c)(ii) and an action is brought subsequent to such determination within such time as may be fixed by the Tribunal.

e) Unless national law provides to the contrary, any person suffering damage caused by a nuclear incident who has brought an action for compensation within the period provided for in this Article may amend his claim in respect of any aggravation of the damage after the expiry of such period: provided that final judgment has not been entered by the competent court.

Article 9

The operator shall not be liable for damage caused by a nuclear incident directly due to an act of armed conflict, hostilities, civil war, insurrection or, except insofar as the legislation of the Contracting Party in whose territory his nuclear installation is situated may provide to the contrary, a grave natural disaster of an exceptional character.

Article 10

a) To cover the liability under this Convention, the operator shall be required to have and maintain insurance or other financial security of the amount established pursuant to Article 7 and of such type and terms as the competent public authority shall specify.

b) No insurer or other financial guarantor shall suspend or cancel the insurance or other financial security provided for in paragraph (a) of this Article without giving notice in writing of at least two months to the competent public authority or insofar as such insurance or other financial security relates to the carriage of nuclear substances, during the period of the carriage in question.

c) The sums provided as insurance, reinsurance, or other financial security may be drawn upon only for compensation for damage caused by a nuclear incident.

Article 11

The nature, form and extent of the compensation, within the limits of this Convention, as well as the equitable distribution thereof, shall be governed by national law.

Article 12

Compensation payable under this Convention, insurance and reinsurance premiums, sums provided as insurance, reinsurance, or other financial security required pursuant to Article 10, and interest and costs referred to in Article 7(g), shall be freely transferable between the monetary areas of the Contracting Parties.

163

Article 13

a) Except as otherwise provided in this Article, jurisdiction over actions under Articles 3, 4, 6(a) and 6(e) shall lie only with the courts of the Contracting Party in whose territory the nuclear incident occurred.

b) Where a nuclear incident occurs outside the territory of the Contracting Parties, or where the place of the nuclear incident cannot be determined with certainty, jurisdiction over such actions shall lie with the courts of the Contracting Party in whose territory the nuclear installation of the operator liable is situated.

c) Where jurisdiction would lie with the courts of more than one Contracting Party by virtue of paragraphs (a) or (b) of this Article, jurisdiction shall lie:

   i) if the nuclear incident occurred partly outside the territory of any Contracting Party and partly in the territory of a single Contracting Party, with the courts of that Contracting Party; and

   ii) in any other case, with the courts of the Contracting Party determined, at the request of a Contracting Party concerned, by the Tribunal referred to in Article 17 as being the most closely related to the case in question.

d) Judgments entered by the competent court under this Article after trial, or by default, shall, when they have become enforceable under the law applied by that court, become enforceable in the territory of any of the other Contracting Parties as soon as the formalities required by the Contracting Party concerned have been complied with. The merits of the case shall not be the subject of further proceedings. The foregoing provisions shall not apply to interim judgments.

e) If an action is brought against a Contracting Party under this Convention, such Contracting Party may not, except in respect of measures of execution, invoke any jurisdictional immunities before the court competent in accordance with this Article.

Article 14

a) This Convention shall be applied without any discrimination based upon nationality, domicile, or residence.

b) "National law" and "national legislation" mean the national law or the national legislation of the court having jurisdiction under this Convention over claims arising out of a nuclear incident, and that law or legislation shall apply to all matters both substantive and procedural not specifically governed by this Convention.

c) That law and legislation shall be applied without any discrimination based upon nationality, domicile, or residence.

Article 15

a) Any Contracting Party may take such measures as it deems necessary to provide for an increase in the amount of compensation specified in this Convention.

b) Insofar as compensation for damage involves public funds and is in excess of the 5 000 000 Special Drawing Rights referred to in Article 7, any such measure in whatever form may be applied under conditions which may derogate from the provisions of this Convention.

Article 16

Decisions taken by the Steering Committee under Articles 1(a)(ii), 1(a)(iii) and 1(b) shall be adopted by mutual agreement of the members representing the Contracting Parties.

Article 17

Any dispute arising between two or more Contracting Parties concerning the interpretation or application of this Convention shall be examined by the Steering Committee and in the absence of friendly settlement shall, upon the request of a Contracting Party concerned, be submitted to the Tribunal established by the Convention of 20 December 1957 on the Establishment of a Security Control in the Field of Nuclear Energy.

Article 18

a) Reservations to one or more of the provisions of this Convention may be made at any time prior to ratification of or accession to this Convention or prior to the time of notification under Article 23 in respect of any territory or territories mentioned in the notification, and shall be admissible only if the terms of these reservations have been expressly accepted by the Signatories.

b) Such acceptance shall not be required from a Signatory which has not itself ratified this Convention within a period of twelve months after the date of notification to it of such reservation by the Secretary-General of the Organisation in accordance with Article 24.

c) Any reservation admitted in accordance with this Article may be withdrawn at any time by notification addressed to the Secretary-General of the Organisation.

Article 19

a) This Convention shall be ratified. Instruments of ratification shall be deposited with the Secretary-General of the Organisation.

b) This Convention shall come into force upon the deposit of instruments of ratification by not less than five of the Signatories. For each Signatory ratifying thereafter, this Convention shall come into force upon the deposit of its instrument of ratification.

Article 20

Amendments to this Convention shall be adopted by mutual agreement of all the Contracting Parties. They shall come into force when ratified or confirmed by two-thirds of the Contracting Parties. For each Contracting Party ratifying or confirming thereafter, they shall come into force at the date of such ratification or confirmation.

Article 21

a) The Government of any Member or Associate country of the Organisation which is not a Signatory to this Convention may accede thereto by notification addressed to the Secretary-General of the Organisation.

b) The Government of any other country which is not a Signatory to this Convention may accede thereto by notification addressed to the Secretary-General of the Organisation and with the unanimous assent of the Contracting Parties. Such accession shall take effect from the date of such assent.

Article 22

a) This Convention shall remain in effect for a period of ten years as from the date of its coming into force. Any Contracting Party may, by giving twelve months' notice to the Secretary-General of the Organisation, terminate the application of this Convention to itself at the end of the period of ten years.

b) This Convention shall, after the period of ten years, remain in force for a period of five years for such Contracting Parties as have not terminated its application in accordance with paragraph (a) of this Article, and thereafter for successive periods of five years for such Contracting Parties as have not terminated its application at the end of one of such periods of five years by giving twelve months' notice to that effect to the Secretary-General of the Organisation.

c) A conference shall be convened by the Secretary-General of the Organisation in order to consider revisions to this Convention after a period of five years as from the date of its coming into force or, at any other time, at the request of a Contracting Party, within six months from the date of such request.

Article 23

a) This Convention shall apply to the metropolitan territories of the Contracting Parties.

b) Any Signatory or Contracting Party may, at the time of signature or ratification of or accession to this Convention or at any later time, notify the Secretary-General of the Organisation that this Convention shall apply to those of its territories, including the territories for whose international relations it is responsible, to which this Convention is not applicable in accordance with paragraph (a) of this Article and which are mentioned in the notification. Any such notification may in respect of any territory or territories mentioned therein be withdrawn by giving twelve months' notice to that effect to the Secretary-General of the Organisation.

c) Any territories of a Contracting Party, including the territories for whose international relations it is responsible, to which this Convention does not apply shall be regarded for the purposes of this Convention as being a territory of a non-Contracting State.

Article 24

The Secretary-General of the Organisation shall give notice to all Signatories and acceding Governments of the receipt of any instrument of ratification, accession, withdrawal, notification under Article 23, and decisions of the Steering Committee under Articles 1(a)(ii), 1(a)(iii) and 1(b). He shall also notify them of the date on which this Convention comes into force, the text of any amendment thereto and of the date on which such amendment comes into force, and any reservation made in accordance with Article 18.

The following reservations were accepted either at the time of signature of the Convention or at the time of signature of the Additional Protocol:

1.6(a) and (c)(i):

Reservation by the Government of the Federal Republic of Germany, the Government of the Republic of Austria and the Government of the Hellenic Republic.

Reservation of the right to provide, by national law, that persons other than the operator may continue to be liable for damage caused by a nuclear incident on condition that these persons are fully covered in respect of their liability, including defence against unjustified actions, by insurance or other financial security obtained by the operator or out of State funds.

2.6(b) and (d):

Reservation by the Government of the Republic of Austria, the Government of the Hellenic Republic, the Government of the Kingdom of Norway and the Government of the Kingdom of Sweden.

Reservation of the right to consider their national legislation which includes provisions equivalent to those included in the international agreements referred to in Article 6(b) as being international agreements within the meaning of Articles, 6(b) and (d).

3.8(a):

Reservation by the Government of the Federal Republic of Germany and the Government of the Republic of Austria.

Reservation of the right to establish, in respect of nuclear incidents occurring in the Federal Republic of Germany and in the Republic of Austria respectively, a period longer than ten years if measures have been taken to cover the liability of the operator in respect of any actions for compensation begun after the expiry of the period of ten years and during such longer period.

4.9:

Reservation by the Government of the Federal Republic of Germany and the Government of the Republic of Austria.

Reservation of the right to provide, in respect of nuclear incidents occurring in the Federal Republic of Germany and in the Republic of Austria respectively, that the operator shall be liable for damage caused by a nuclear incident directly due to an act of armed conflict, hostilities, civil war, insurrection or a grave natural disaster of an exceptional character.

5.19 :

Reservation by the Government of the Federal Republic of Germany, the Government of the Republic of Austria, and the Government of the Hellenic Republic.

Reservation of the right to consider ratification of this Convention as constituting an obligation under international law to enact national legislation on third party liability in the field of nuclear energy in accordance with the provisions of this Convention.

ANNEX II

This Convention shall not be interpreted as depriving a Contracting Party, on whose territory damage was caused by a nuclear incident occurring on the territory of another Contracting Party, of any recourse which might be available to it under international law.

IN WITNESS WHEREOF, the undersigned Plenipotentiaries, duly empowered, have signed this Convention.

DONE in Paris, this twenty-ninth day of July Nineteen Hundred and Sixty, in the English, French, German, Spanish, Italian and Dutch languages in a single copy which shall remain deposited with the Secretary-General of the Organisation for European Economic Co-operation by whom certified copies will be communicated to all Signatories.

BRUSSELS CONVENTION OF 31 JANUARY 1963 SUPPLEMENTARY TO THE *PARIS CONVENTION OF 29 JULY 1960*, AS AMENDED BY *THE ADDITIONAL PROTOCOL OF 28 JANUARY 1964* AND BY THE *PROTOCOL OF 16 NOVEMBER 1982*

THE GOVERNMENTS of the Federal Republic of Germany, the Republic of Austria, the Kingdom of Belgium, the Kingdom of Denmark, the Kingdom of Spain, the Republic of Finland, the French Republic, the Italian Republic, the Grand Duchy of Luxembourg, the Kingdom of Norway, the Kingdom of the Netherlands, the United Kingdom of Great Britain and Northern Ireland, the Kingdom of Sweden and the Swiss Confederation,

BEING PARTIES to the Convention of 29 July 1960 on Third Party Liability in the Field of Nuclear Energy, concluded within the framework of the Organisation for European Economic Co-operation, now the Organisation for Economic Co-operation and Development, and as amended by the Additional Protocol concluded at Paris on 16 November 1982 (hereinafter referred to as the "*Paris Convention*");

DESIROUS of supplementing the measures provided in that Convention with a view to increasing the amount of compensation for damage which might result from the use of nuclear energy for peaceful purposes;

HAVE AGREED as follows:

Article 1

The system instituted by this Convention is supplementary to that of the *Paris Convention*, shall be subject to the provisions of the *Paris Convention*, and shall be applied in accordance with the following Articles.

Article 2

a)   The system of this Convention shall apply to damage caused by nuclear incidents, other than those occurring entirely in the territory of a State which is not a Party to this Convention:

i) for which an operator of a nuclear installation, used for peaceful purposes, situated in the territory of a Contracting Party to this Convention (hereinafter referred to as a "Contracting Party"), and which appears on the list established and kept up to date in accordance with the terms of Article 13, is liable under the *Paris Convention*; and

ii) suffered

   1. in the territory of a Contracting Party; or

   2. on or over the high seas on board a ship or aircraft registered in the territory of a Contracting Party; or

   3. on or over the high seas by a national of a Contracting Party, provided that, in the case of damage to a ship or an aircraft, the ship or aircraft is registered in the territory of a Contracting Party,

provided that the courts of a Contracting Party have jurisdiction pursuant to the *Paris Convention*.

b) Any Signatory or acceding Government may, at the time of signature of or accession to this Convention or on the deposit of its instrument of ratification, declare that, for the purposes of the application of paragraph (a) (ii) (3) of this Article, individuals or certain categories thereof, considered under its law as having their habitual residence in its territory, are assimilated to its own nationals.

c) In this Article, the expression "a national of a Contracting Party" shall include a Contracting Party or any of its constituent subdivisions, or a partnership, or any public or private body whether corporate or not established in the territory of a Contracting Party.

Article 3

a) Under the conditions established by this Convention, the Contracting Parties undertake that compensation in respect of the damage referred to in Article 2 shall be provided up to the amount of 300 million Special Drawing Rights per incident.

b) Such compensation shall be provided:

i) up to an amount of at least 5 million Special Drawing Rights, out of funds provided by insurance or other financial security, such amount to be established by the legislation of the Contracting Party in whose territory the nuclear installation of the operator liable is situated;

ii) between this amount and 175 million Special Drawing Rights, out of public funds to be made available by the Contracting Party in whose territory the nuclear installation of the operator liable is situated;

iii) between 175 and 300 million Special Drawing Rights, out of public funds to be made available by the Contracting Parties according to the formula for contributions specified in Article 12.

c) For this purpose, each Contracting Party shall either:

i) establish the maximum liability of the operator, pursuant to Article 7 of the *Paris Convention*, at 300 million Special Drawing Rights, and provide that such liability shall be covered by all the funds referred to in paragraph (b) of this Article; or

ii) establish the maximum liability of the operator at an amount at least equal to that established pursuant to paragraph (b)(i) of this Article and provide that, in excess of such amount and up to 300 million Special Drawing Rights, the public funds referred to in paragraphs (b)(ii) and (iii) of this Article shall be made available by some means other than as cover for the liability of the operator, provided that the rules of substance and procedure laid down in this Convention are not thereby affected.

d) The obligation of the operator to pay compensation, interest or costs out of public funds made available pursuant to paragraphs (b)(ii) and (iii), and (f) of this Article shall only be enforceable against the operator as and when such funds are in fact made available.

e) The Contracting Parties, in carrying out this Convention, undertake not to make use of the right provided for in Article 15(b) of the *Paris Convention* to apply special conditions:

i) in respect of compensation for damage provided out of the funds referred to in paragraph (b)(i) of this Article;

ii) other than those laid down in this Convention in respect of compensation for damage provided out of the public funds referred to in paragraphs (b)(ii) and (iii) of this Article.

f) The interest and costs referred to in Article 7(g) of the *Paris Convention* are payable in addition to the amounts referred to in paragraph (b) of this Article and shall be borne insofar as they are awarded in respect of compensation payable out of the funds referred to in:

i) paragraph (b)(i) of this Article, by the operator liable;

ii) paragraph (b)(ii) of this Article, by the Contracting Party in whose territory the nuclear installation of that operator is situated;

iii) paragraph (b)(iii) of this Article, by the Contracting Parties together.

g) For the purposes of this Convention, "Special Drawing Right" means the Special Drawing Right as it is defined by the International Monetary Fund. The amounts mentioned in this Convention shall be converted into the national currency of a Contracting Party in accordance with the value of that currency at the date of the incident, unless another date is fixed for a given incident by agreement between the Contracting Parties. The equivalent in Special Drawing Rights of the national currency of a Contracting Party shall be calculated in accordance with the method of valuation applied at the date in question by the International Monetary Fund for its own operations and transactions.

Article 4

a) If a nuclear incident causes damage which gives rise to liability of more than one operator, the aggregate liability provided for in Article 5(d) of the *Paris Convention* shall not, to the extent that public funds have to be made available pursuant to Articles 3(b)(ii) and (iii), exceed 300 million Special Drawing Rights.

b) The total amount of the public funds made available pursuant to Articles 3(b)(ii) and (iii) shall not, in such event, exceed the difference between 300 million Special Drawing Rights and the sum of the amounts established with respect to such operators pursuant to Article 3(b)(i) or, in the case of an operator whose nuclear installation is situated in the territory of a State which is not a Party to this Convention, the amount established pursuant to Article 7 of the *Paris Convention*. If more than one Contracting Party is required to make available public funds pursuant to Article 3(b)(ii), such funds shall be made available by them in proportion to the number of nuclear installations situated in their respective territories, which are involved in the nuclear incident and of which the operators are liable.

Article 5

a) Where the operator liable has a right of recourse pursuant to Article 6(f) of the *Paris Convention*, the Contracting Party in whose territory the nuclear installation of that operator is situated shall take such legislative measures as are necessary to enable both that Contracting Party and the other Contracting Parties to benefit from this recourse to the extent that public funds have been made available pursuant to Articles 3(b)(ii) and (iii), and (f).

b) Such legislation may provide for the recovery of public funds made available pursuant to Articles 3(b)(ii) and (iii), and (f) from such operator if the damage results from fault on his part.

Article 6

In calculating the public funds to be made available pursuant to this Convention, account shall be taken only of those rights to compensation exercised within ten years from the date of the nuclear incident. In the case of damage caused by a nuclear incident involving nuclear fuel or radioactive products or waste which, at the time of the incident have been stolen, lost, jettisoned, or abandoned and have not yet been recovered, such period shall not in any case exceed twenty years from the date of the theft, loss, jettison or abandonment. It shall also be extended in the cases and under the conditions laid down in Article 8(d) of the *Paris Convention*. Amendments made to claims after the expiry of this period, under the conditions laid down in Article 8(e) of the *Paris Convention*, shall also be taken into account.

Article 7

Where a Contracting Party makes use of the right provided for in Article 8(c) of the *Paris Convention*, the period which it establishes shall be a period of prescription of three years either from the date at which the person suffering damage has knowledge or from the date at which he ought reasonably to have known of both the damage and the operator liable.

Article 8

Any person who is entitled to benefit from the provisions of this Convention shall have the right to full compensation in accordance with national law for damage suffered: provided that, where the amount of damage exceeds or is likely to exceed:

    i) 300 million Special Drawing Rights; or

    ii) if there is aggregate liability under Article 5(d) of the *Paris Convention* and a higher sum results therefrom, such higher sum,

any Contracting Party may establish equitable criteria for apportionment. Such criteria shall be applied whatever the origin of the funds and, subject to the provisions of Article 2, without discrimination based on the nationality, domicile, or residence of the person suffering the damage.

Article 9

a)   The system of disbursements by which the public funds required under Articles 3(b)(ii) and (iii), and (f) are to be made available shall be that of the Contracting Party whose courts have jurisdiction.

b) Each Contracting Party shall ensure that persons suffering damage may enforce their rights to compensation without having to bring separate proceedings according to the origin of the funds provided for such compensation.

c) No Contracting Party shall be required to make available the public funds referred to in Articles 3(b)(ii) and (iii) so long as any of the funds referred to in Article 3(b)(i) remain available.

Article 10

a) The Contracting Party whose courts have jurisdiction shall be required to inform the other Contracting Parties of a nuclear incident and its circumstances as soon as it appears that the damage caused by such incident exceeds, or is likely to exceed, 175 million Special Drawing Rights. The Contracting Parties shall without delay make all the necessary arrangements to settle the procedure for their relations in this connection.

b) Only the Contracting Party whose courts have jurisdiction shall be entitled to request the other Contracting Parties to make available the public funds required under Articles 3(b)(iii) and (f) and shall have exclusive competence to disburse such funds.

c) Such Contracting Party shall, when the occasion arises, exercise the right of recourse provided for in Article 5 on behalf of the other Contracting Parties who have made available public funds pursuant to Articles 3(b)(iii) and (f).

d) Settlements effected in respect of the payment of compensation out of the public funds referred to in Articles 3(b)(ii) and (iii) in accordance with the conditions established by national legislation shall be recognised by the other Contracting Parties, and judgments entered by the competent courts in respect of such compensation shall become enforceable in the territory of the other Contracting Parties in accordance with the provisions of Article 13(d) of the *Paris Convention*.

Article 11

a) If the courts having jurisdiction are those of a Contracting Party other than the Contracting Party in whose territory the nuclear installation of the operator liable is situated, the public funds required under Articles 3(b)(ii) and (f) shall be made available by the first-named Contracting Party. The Contracting Party in whose territory the nuclear installation of the operator liable is situated shall reimburse to the other Contracting Party the sums paid. These two Contracting Parties shall agree on the procedure for reimbursement.

b)   In adopting all legislative, regulatory or administrative provisions, after the nuclear incident has occurred, concerning the nature, form and extent of the compensation, the procedure for making available the public funds required under Article 3(b)(ii) and, if necessary, the criteria for the apportionment of such funds, the Contracting Party whose courts have jurisdiction shall consult the Contracting Party in whose territory the nuclear installation of the operator liable is situated. It shall further take all measures necessary to enable the latter to intervene in proceedings and to participate in any settlement concerning compensation.

Article 12

a)   The formula for contributions according to which the Contracting Parties shall make available the public funds referred to in Article 3(b)(iii) shall be determined as follows:

i)   as to 50%, on the basis of the ratio between the gross national product at current prices of each Contracting Party and the total of the gross national products at current prices of all Contracting Parties as shown by the official statistics published by the Organisation for Economic Co-operation and Development for the year preceding the year in which the nuclear incident occurs;

ii)   as to 50%, on the basis of the ratio between the thermal power of the reactors situated in the territory of each Contracting Party and the total thermal power of the reactors situated in the territories of all the Contracting Parties. This calculation shall be made on the basis of the thermal power of the reactors shown at the date of the nuclear incident in the list referred to in Article 2(a)(i): provided that a reactor shall only be taken into consideration for the purposes of this calculation as from the date when it first reaches criticality.

b)   For the purposes of this Convention, "thermal power" means:

i)   before the issue of a final operating licence, the planned thermal power;

ii)   after the issue of such licence, the thermal power authorised by the competent national authorities.

Article 13

a)   Each Contracting Party shall ensure that all nuclear installations used for peaceful purposes situated in its territory, and falling within the definition in Article 1 of the *Paris Convention*, appear on the list referred to in Article 2(a)(i).

b)   For this purpose, each Signatory or acceding Government shall, on the deposit of its instrument of ratification or accession, communicate to the Belgian Government full particulars of such installations.

c)   Such particulars shall indicate:

   i)   in the case of all installations not yet completed, the expected date on which the risk of a nuclear incident will exist;

   ii) and further, in the case of reactors, the expected date on which they will first reach criticality, and also their thermal power.

d)   Each Contracting Party shall also communicate to the Belgian Government the exact date of the existence of the risk of a nuclear incident and, in the case of reactors, the date on which they first reached criticality.

e)   Each Contracting Party shall also communicate to the Belgian Government all modifications to be made to the list. Where such modifications include the addition of a nuclear installation, the communication must be made at least three months before the expected date on which the risk of a nuclear incident will exist.

f)   If a Contracting Party is of the opinion that the particulars, or any modification to be made to the list, communicated by another Contracting Party do not comply with the provisions of Article 2(a)(i) and of this Article, it may raise objections thereto only by addressing them to the Belgian Government within three months from the date on which it has received notice pursuant to paragraph (h) of this Article.

g)   If a Contracting Party is of the opinion that a communication required in accordance with this Article has not been made within the time prescribed in this Article, it may raise objections only by addressing them to the Belgian Government within three months from the date on which it knew of the facts which, in its opinion, ought to have been communicated.

h)   The Belgian Government shall give notice as soon as possible to each Contracting Party of the communications and objections which it has received pursuant to this Article.

i)   The list referred to in Article 2(a)(i) shall consist of all the particulars and modifications referred to in paragraphs (b), (c), (d) and (e) of this Article, it being understood that objections submitted pursuant to paragraphs (f) and (g) of this Article shall have effect retrospective to the date on which they were raised, if they are sustained.

j) The Belgian Government shall supply any Contracting Party on demand with an up-to-date statement of the nuclear installations covered by this Convention and the details supplied in respect of them pursuant to this Article.

Article 14

a) Except insofar as this Convention otherwise provides, each Contracting Party may exercise the powers vested in it by virtue of the *Paris Convention*, and any provisions made thereunder may be invoked against the other Contracting Parties in order that the public funds referred to in Articles 3(b)(ii) and (iii) be made available.

b) Any such provisions made by a Contracting Party pursuant to Articles 2 and 9 of the *Paris Convention* as a result of which the public funds referred to in Articles 3(b)(ii) and (iii) are required to be made available may not be invoked against any other Contracting Party unless it has consented thereto.

c) Nothing in this Convention shall prevent a Contracting Party from making provisions outside the scope of the *Paris Convention* and of this Convention, provided that such provisions shall not involve any further obligation on the part of the Contracting Parties insofar as their public funds are concerned.

Article 15

a) Any Contracting Party may conclude an agreement with a State which is not a Party to this Convention concerning compensation out of public funds for damage caused by a nuclear incident.

b) To the extent that the conditions for payment of compensation under any such agreement are not more favourable than those which result from the measures adopted by the Contracting Party concerned for the application of the *Paris Convention* and of this Convention, the amount of damage caused by a nuclear incident covered by this Convention and for which compensation is payable by virtue of such an agreement may be taken into consideration, where the proviso to Article 8 applies, in calculating the total amount of damage caused by that incident.

c) The provisions of paragraphs (a) and (b) of this Article shall in no case affect the obligations under Articles 3(b)(ii) and (iii) of those Contracting Parties which have not given their consent to such agreement.

d) Any Contracting Party intending to conclude such an agreement shall notify the other Contracting Parties of its intention. Agreements concluded shall be notified to the Belgian Government.

Article 16

a) The Contracting Parties shall consult each other upon all problems of common interest raised by the application of this Convention and of the *Paris Convention*, especially Articles 20 and 22(c) of the latter Convention.

b) They shall consult each other on the desirability of revising this Convention after a period of five years from the date of its coming into force, and at any other time upon the request of a Contracting Party.

Article 17

Any dispute arising between two or more Contracting Parties concerning the interpretation or application of this Convention shall, upon the request of a Contracting Party concerned, be submitted to the European Nuclear Energy Tribunal established by the *Convention of 20 December 1957 on the Establishment of a Security Control in the Field of Nuclear Energy*.

Article 18

a) Reservations to one or more of the provisions of this Convention may be made at any time prior to ratification of this Convention if the terms of these reservations have been expressly accepted by all Signatories or, at the time of accession or of application of the provisions of Articles 21 and 24, if the terms of these reservations have been expressly accepted by all Signatories and acceding Governments.

b) Such acceptance shall not be required from a Signatory which has not itself ratified this Convention within a period of twelve months after the date of notification to it of such reservation by the Belgian Government in accordance with Article 25.

c) Any reservation accepted in accordance with the provisions of paragraph (a) of this Article may be withdrawn at any time by notification addressed to the Belgian Government.

Article 19

No State may become or continue to be a Contracting Party to this Convention unless it is a Contracting Party to the *Paris Convention*.

Article 20

a) The Annex to this Convention shall form an integral part thereof.

b) This Convention shall be ratified. Instruments of ratification shall be deposited with the Belgian Government.

c) This Convention shall come into force three months after the deposit of the sixth instrument of ratification.

d) For each Signatory ratifying this Convention after the deposit of the sixth instrument of ratification, it shall come into force three months after the date of the deposit of its instrument of ratification.

Article 21

Amendments to this Convention shall be adopted by agreement among all the Contracting Parties. They shall come into force on the date when all Contracting Parties have ratified or confirmed them.

Article 22

a) After the coming into force of this Convention, any Contracting Party to the *Paris Convention* which has not signed this Convention may request accession to this Convention by notification addressed to the Belgian Government.

b) Such accession shall require the unanimous assent of the Contracting Parties.

c) Once such assent has been given, the Contracting Party to the *Paris Convention* requesting accession shall deposit its instrument of accession with the Belgian Government.

d) The accession shall take effect three months from the date of deposit of the instrument of accession.

Article 23

a)   This Convention shall remain in force until the expiry of the *Paris Convention*.

b)   Any Contracting Party may, by giving twelve months' notice to the Belgian Government, terminate the application of this Convention to itself after the end of the period of ten years specified in Article 22(a) of the *Paris Convention*. Within six months after receipt of such notice, any other Contracting Party may, by notice to the Belgian Government, terminate the application of this Convention to itself as from the date when it ceases to have effect in respect of the Contracting Party which first gave notice.

c)   The expiry of this Convention or the withdrawal of a Contracting Party shall not terminate the obligations assumed by each Contracting Party under this Convention to pay compensation for damage caused by nuclear incidents occurring before the date of such expiry or withdrawal.

d)   The Contracting Parties shall, in good time, consult each other on what measures should be taken after the expiry of this Convention or the withdrawal of one or more of the Contracting Parties, to provide compensation comparable to that accorded by this Convention for damage caused by nuclear incidents occurring after the date of such expiry or withdrawal and for which the operator of a nuclear installation in operation before such date within the territories of the Contracting Parties is liable.

Article 24

a)   This Convention shall apply to the metropolitan territories of the Contracting Parties.

b)   Any Contracting Party desiring the application of this Convention to one or more of the territories in respect of which, pursuant to Article 23 of the *Paris Convention*, it has given notification of application of that Convention, shall address a request to the Belgian Government.

c)   The application of this Convention to any such territory shall require the unanimous assent of the Contracting Parties.

d)   Once such assent has been given, the Contracting Party concerned shall address to the Belgian Government a notification which shall take effect as from the date of its receipt.

e)   Such notification may, as regards any territory mentioned therein, be withdrawn by the Contracting Party which has made it by giving twelve months' notice to that effect to the Belgian Government.

f)   If the *Paris Convention* ceases to apply to any such territory, this Convention shall also cease to apply thereto.

Article 25

The Belgian Government shall notify all Signatories and acceding Governments of the receipt of any instrument of ratification, accession or withdrawal, and shall also notify them of the date on which this Convention comes into force, the text of any amendment thereto and the date on which such amendment comes into force, any reservations made in accordance with Article 18, and all notifications which it has received.

IN WITNESS WHEREOF the undersigned Plenipotentiaries, duly empowered, have signed this Convention.

DONE at Brussels, this 31st day of January 1963, in the English, Dutch, French, German, Italian and Spanish languages, the six texts being equally authoritative, in a single copy which shall be deposited with the Belgian Government by whom certified copies shall be communicated to all the other Signatories and acceding Governments.

TO THE CONVENTION OF 31 JANUARY 1963
SUPPLEMENTARY TO THE *PARIS CONVENTION OF 29 JULY 1960*
ON THIRD PARTY LIABILITY IN THE FIELD OF NUCLEAR ENERGY,
AS AMENDED BY THE *ADDITIONAL PROTOCOL OF 28 JANUARY 1964*
AND BY THE *PROTOCOL OF 16 NOVEMBER 1982*

THE GOVERNMENTS OF THE CONTRACTING PARTIES declare that compensation for damage caused by a nuclear incident not covered by the Supplementary Convention solely by reason of the fact that the relevant nuclear installation, on account of its utilisation, is not on the list referred to in Article 2 of the Supplementary Convention, (including the case where such installation is considered by one or more but not all of the Governments to be outside the *Paris Convention*):

–   shall be provided without discrimination among the nationals of the Contracting Parties to the Supplementary Convention; and

–   shall not be limited to less than 300 million Special Drawing Rights.

In addition, if they have not already done so, they shall endeavour to make the rules for compensation of persons suffering damage caused by such incidents as similar as possible to those established in respect of nuclear incidents occurring in connection with nuclear installations covered by the Supplementary Convention.

VIENNA CONVENTION ON
CIVIL LIABILITY FOR NUCLEAR DAMAGE
OF 21 MAY 1963

THE CONTRACTING PARTIES,

HAVING RECOGNISED the desirability of establishing some minimum standards to provide financial protection against damage resulting from certain peaceful uses of nuclear energy;

BELIEVING that a convention on civil liability for nuclear damage would also contribute to the development of friendly relations among nations, irrespective of their differing constitutional and social systems;

HAVE DECIDED to conclude a convention for such purposes, and thereto have agreed as follows:

ARTICLE I

1. For the purposes of this Convention:

(a) "person" means any individual, partnership, any private or public body whether corporate or not, any international organisation enjoying legal personality under the law of the Installation State, and any State or any of its constituent subdivisions;

(b) "national of a Contracting Party" includes a Contracting Party or any of its constituent subdivisions, a partnership, or any private or public body whether corporate or not established within the territory of a Contracting Party;

(c) "operator", in relation to a nuclear installation, means the person designated or recognized by the Installation State as the operator of the installation;

(d) "installation State", in relation to a nuclear installation, means the Contracting Party within whose territory that installation is situated or, if it is not situated within the territory of any State, the Contracting Party by which or under the authority of which the nuclear installation is operated;

(e) "law of the competent court" means the law of the court having jurisdiction under this Convention, including any rules of such laws;

(f) "nuclear fuel" means any material which is capable of producing energy by a self-sustaining chain process of nuclear fission;

(g) "radioactive products or waste" means any radioactive material produced in, or any material made radioactive by exposure to the radiation incidental to, the production or utilisation of nuclear fuel, but does not include radioisotopes which have reached the final stage of fabrication so as to be usable for any scientific, medical, agricultural, commercial or industrial purpose;

(h) "nuclear material" means:

    (i) nuclear fuel, other than natural uranium and depleted uranium capable of producing energy by a self-sustaining chain process of nuclear fission outside a nuclear reactor, either alone or in combination with some other material; and

    (ii) radioactive products or waste;

(i) "nuclear reactor" means any structure containing nuclear fuel in such an arrangement that a self-sustaining chain process of nuclear fission can occur therein without an additional source of neutrons.

(j) "nuclear installation" means:

    (i) any nuclear reactor other than one with which a means of sea or air transport is equipped for use as a source of power, whether for propulsion thereof or for any other purpose;

    (ii) any factory using nuclear fuel for the production of nuclear material, or any factory for the processing of nuclear material, including any factory for the reprocessing or irradiated nuclear fuel; and

    (iii) any facility where nuclear material is stored, other than storage incidental to the carriage of such material;

provided that the installation State may determine that several nuclear installations of one operator which are located at the same site shall be considered as a single nuclear installation;

(k) "nuclear damage" means:

    (i) loss of life, any personal injury or any loss of, or damage to, property which arises out of or results from the radioactive properties or a combination of radioactive properties with toxic, explosive or other hazardous properties of nuclear fuel or radioactive products or waste in, or of nuclear material coming from, originating in, or sent to, a nuclear installation;

(ii) any other loss or damage so arising or resulting if and to the extent that the law of the competent court so provides; and

(iii) if the law of the Installation State so provides, loss of life, any personal injury or any loss of, or damage to, property which arises out of or results from other ionising radiation emitted by any other source of radiation inside a nuclear installation; and

(l) "nuclear incident" means any occurrence or series of occurrences having the same origin which causes nuclear damage.

2. An installation State may, if the small extent of the risks involved so warrants, exclude any small quantities of nuclear material from the application of this Convention, provided that:

(a) maximum limits for the exclusion of such quantities have been established by the Board of Governors of the International Atomic Energy Agency; and

(b) any exclusion by the installation State is within such established limits.

The maximum limits shall be reviewed periodically by the Board of Governors.

Article II

1. The operator of a nuclear installation shall be liable for nuclear damage upon proof that such damage has been caused by a nuclear incident:

(a) in his nuclear installation; or

(b) involving nuclear material coming from or originating in his nuclear installation, and occurring:

(i) before liability with regard to nuclear incidents involving the nuclear material has been assumed, pursuant to the express terms of a contract in writing, by the operator of another nuclear installation;

(ii) in the absence of such express terms, before the operator of another nuclear installation has taken charge of the nuclear material; or

(iii) where the nuclear material is intended to be used in a nuclear reactor with which a means of transport is equipped for use as a source of power, whether for propulsion thereof or for any other purpose, before the person duly authorised to operate such reactor has taken charge of the nuclear material; but

(iv) where the nuclear material has been sent to a person within the territory of a non-Contracting State;

(c)   involving nuclear material sent to his nuclear installation, and occurring:

(i)   after liability with regard to nuclear incidents involving the nuclear material has been assumed by him, pursuant to the express terms of a contract in writing, from the operator of another nuclear installation;

(ii) in the absence of such express terms, after he has taken charge of the nuclear material; or

(iii) after he has taken charge of the nuclear material from a person operating a nuclear reactor with which a means of transport is equipped for use as a source of power, whether for propulsion thereof or for any other purpose; but

(iv) where the nuclear material has, with the written consent of the operator, been sent from a person within the territory of a non-Contracting State, only after it has been loaded on the means of transport by which it is to be carried from the territory of that State;

provided that, if nuclear damage is caused by a nuclear incident occurring in a nuclear installation and involving nuclear material stored therein incidentally to the carriage of such material, the provisions of subparagraph (a) of this paragraph shall not apply where another operator or person is solely liable pursuant to the provisions of subparagraphs (b) or (c) of this paragraph.

2. The Installation State may provide by legislation that, in accordance with such terms as may be specified therein, a carrier of nuclear material or a person handling radioactive waste may, at his request and with the consent of the operator concerned, be designated or recognised as operator in the place of that operator in respect of such nuclear material or radioactive waste respectively. In this case such carrier or such person shall be considered, for all the purposes of this Convention, as an operator of a nuclear installation situated within the territory of that State.

3. (a) Where nuclear damage engages the liability of more than one operator, the operators involved shall, insofar as the damage attributable to each operator is not reasonably separable, be jointly and severally liable.

(b) Where a nuclear incident occurs in the course of carriage of nuclear material, either in one and the same means of transport, or, in the case of storage incidental to the carriage, in one and the same nuclear installation, and causes nuclear damage which engages the liability of more than one operator, the total liability shall not exceed the highest amount applicable with respect to any one of them pursuant to Article V.

(c) In neither of the cases referred to in subparagraphs (a) and (b) of this paragraph shall the liability of any one operator exceed the amount applicable with respect to him pursuant to Article V.

4. Subject to the provisions of paragraph 3 of this Article, where several nuclear installations of one and the same operator are involved in one nuclear incident, such operator shall be liable in respect of each nuclear installation involved up to the amount applicable with respect to him pursuant to Article V.

5. Except as otherwise provided in this Convention, no person other than the operator shall be liable for nuclear damage. This, however, shall not affect the application of any international convention in the field of transport in force or open for signature, ratification or accession at the date on which this Convention is opened for signature.

6. No person shall be liable for any loss or damage which is not nuclear damage pursuant to subparagraph (k) of paragraph 1 of Article I but which should have been included as such pursuant to sub-paragraph (k)(ii) of that paragraph.

7. Direct action shall lie against the person furnishing financial security pursuant to Article VII, if the law of the competent court so provides.

Article III

The operator liable in accordance with this Convention shall provide the carrier with a certificate issued by or on behalf of the insurer or other financial guarantor furnishing the financial security required pursuant to Article VII. The certificate shall state the name and address of that operator and the amount, type and duration of the security, and these statements may not be disputed by the person by whom or on whose behalf the certificate was issued. The certificate shall also indicate the nuclear material in respect of which the security applies and shall include a statement by the competent public authority of the Installation State that the person named is an operator within the meaning of this Convention.

Article IV

1. The liability of the operator for nuclear damage under this Convention shall be absolute.

2. If the operator proves that the nuclear damage resulted wholly or partly either from the gross negligence of the person suffering the damage or from an act or omission of such person done with intent to cause damage, the competent court may, if its law so provides, relieve the operator wholly or partly from his obligation to pay compensation in respect of the damage suffered by such person.

3. (a) No liability under this Convention shall attach to an operator for nuclear damage caused by a nuclear incident directly due to an act of armed conflict, hostilities, civil war or insurrection.

(b) Except insofar as the law of the Installation State may provide to the contrary, the operator shall not be liable for nuclear damage caused by a nuclear incident directly due to a grave natural disaster of an exceptional character.

4. Whenever both nuclear damage and damage other than nuclear damage have been caused by a nuclear incident or jointly by a nuclear incident and one or more other occurrences, such other damage shall, to the extent that it is not reasonably separable from the nuclear damage, be deemed, for the purposes of this Convention, to be nuclear damage caused by that nuclear incident. Where, however, damage is caused jointly by a nuclear incident covered by this Convention and by an emission of ionising radiation not covered by it, nothing in this Convention shall limit or otherwise affect the liability, either as regards any person suffering nuclear damage or by way of recourse or contribution, of any person who may be held liable in connection with that emission of ionising radiation.

5. The operator shall not be liable under this Convention for nuclear damage:

(a) to the nuclear installation itself or to any property on the site of that installation which is used or to be used in connection with that installation; or

(b) to the means of transport upon which the nuclear material involved was at the time of the nuclear incident.

6. Any Installation State may provide by legislation that subparagraph (b) of paragraph 5 of this Article shall not apply, provided that in no case shall the liability of the operator in respect of nuclear damage, other than nuclear damage to the means of transport, be reduced to less than US $5 million for any one nuclear incident.

7. Nothing in this Convention shall affect:

(a) the liability of any individual for nuclear damage for which the operator, by virtue of paragraphs 3 or 5 of this Article, is not liable under this Convention and which that individual caused by an act or omission done with intent to cause damage; or

(b) the liability outside this Convention of the operator for nuclear damage for which, by virtue of subparagraph (b) of paragraph 5 of this Article, he is not liable under this Convention.

Article V

1. The liability of the operator may be limited by the Installation State to not less than US $5 million for any one nuclear incident.

2. Any limits of liability which may be established pursuant to this Article shall not include any interest or costs awarded by a court in actions for compensation of nuclear damage.

3. The United States dollar referred to in this Convention is a unit of account equivalent to the value of the United States dollar in terms of gold on 29 April 1963, that is to say US $35 per one troy ounce of fine gold.

4. The sum mentioned in paragraph 6 of Article IV and in paragraph 1 of this Article may be converted into national currency in round figures.

Article VI

1. Rights of compensation under this Convention shall be extinguished if an action is not brought within ten years from the date of the nuclear incident. If, however, under the law of the Installation State the liability of the operator is covered by insurance or other financial security or by State funds for a period longer than ten years, the law of the competent court may provide that rights of compensation against the operator shall only be extinguished after a period which may be longer than ten years, but shall not be longer than the period for which his liability is so covered under the law of the Installation State. Such extension of the extinction period shall in no case affect rights of compensation under this Convention of any person who has brought an action for loss of life or personal injury against the operator before the expiry of the aforesaid period of ten years.

2. Where nuclear damage is caused by a nuclear incident involving nuclear material which at the time of the nuclear incident was stolen, lost, jettisoned or abandoned, the period established pursuant to paragraph 1 of this Article shall be computed from the date of that nuclear incident, but the period shall in no case exceed a period of twenty years from the date of the theft, loss, jettison or abandonment.

3. The law of the competent court may establish a period of extinction or prescription of not less than three years from the date on which the person suffering nuclear damage had knowledge or should have had knowledge of the damage and of the

operator liable for the damage, provided that the period established pursuant to paragraphs 1 and 2 of this Article shall not be exceeded.

4. Unless the law of the competent court otherwise provides, any person who claims to have suffered nuclear damage and who has brought an action for compensation within the period applicable pursuant to this Article may amend his claim to take into account any aggravation of the damage, even after the expiry of that period, provided that final judgment has not been entered.

5. Where jurisdiction is to be determined pursuant to subparagraph (b) of paragraph 3 of Article XI and a request has been made within the period applicable pursuant to this Article to any one of the Contracting Parties empowered so to determine, but the time remaining after such determination is less than six months, the period within which an action may be brought shall be six months, reckoned from the date of such determination.

Article VII

1. The operator shall be required to maintain insurance or other financial security covering his liability for nuclear damage in such amount, of such type and in such terms as the Installation State shall specify. The Installation State shall ensure the payment of claims for compensation for nuclear damage which have been established against the operator by providing the necessary funds to the extent that the yield of insurance or other financial security is inadequate to satisfy such claims, but not in excess of the limits, if any, established pursuant to Article V.

2. Nothing in paragraph 1 of this Article shall require a Contracting Party or any of its constituent subdivisions, such as States or Republics, to maintain insurance or other financial security to cover their liability as operators.

3. The funds provided by insurance, by other financial security or by the Installation State pursuant to paragraph 1 of this Article shall be exclusively available for compensation due under this Convention.

4. No insurer or other financial guarantor shall suspend or cancel the insurance or other financial security provided pursuant to paragraph 1 of this Article without giving notice in writing of at least two months to the competent public authority or, insofar as such insurance or other financial security relates to the carriage of nuclear material, during the period of the carriage in question.

Article VIII

Subject to the provisions of this Convention, the nature, form and extent of the compensation, as well as the equitable distribution thereof, shall be governed by the law of the competent court.

Article IX

1.   Where provisions of national or public health insurance, social insurance, social security, workmen's compensation or occupational disease compensation systems include compensation for nuclear damage, rights of beneficiaries of such systems to obtain compensation under this Convention and rights of recourse by virtue of such systems against the operator liable shall be determined, subject to the provisions of this Convention, by the law of the Contracting Party in which such systems have been established, or by the regulations of the intergovernmental organization which has established such systems.

2. (a)   If a person who is a national or a Contracting Party, other than the operator, has paid compensation for nuclear damage under an international convention or under the law of a non-Contracting State, such person shall, up to the amount which he had paid, acquire by subrogation the rights under this Convention of the person so compensated. No rights shall be so acquired by any person to the extent that the operator has a right of recourse against such person under this Convention.

(b)   Nothing in this Convention shall preclude an operator who has paid compensation for nuclear damage out of funds other than those provided pursuant to paragraph 1 of Article VII from recovering from the person providing financial security pursuant to that paragraph or from the Installation State, up to the amount he has paid, the sum which the person so compensated would have obtained under this Convention.

Article X

The operator shall have a right of recourse only:

(a)   if this is expressly provided for by a contract in writing; or

(b)   if the nuclear incident results from an act or omission done with intent to cause damage, against the individual who has acted or omitted to act with such intent.

Article XI

1.   Except as otherwise provided in this Article, jurisdiction over actions under Article II shall lie only with the courts of the Contracting Party within whose territory the nuclear incident occurred.

2.   Where the nuclear incident occurred outside the territory of any Contracting Party, or where the place of the nuclear incident cannot be determined with certainty, jurisdiction over such actions shall lie with the courts of the Installation State of the operator liable.

3. Where under paragraphs 1 or 2 of this Article jurisdiction would lie with the courts of more than one Contracting Party, jurisdiction shall lie:

    (a) if the nuclear incident occurred partly outside the territory of any Contracting Party, and partly within the territory of a single Contracting Party, with the courts of the latter; and

    (b) in any other case, with the courts of that Contracting Party which is determined by agreement between the Contracting Parties whose courts would be competent under paragraphs 1 or 2 of this Article.

Article XII

1. A final judgment entered by a court having jurisdiction under Article XI shall be recognised within the territory of any other Contracting Party, except:

    (a) where the judgment was obtained by fraud;

    (b) where the party against whom the judgment was pronounced was not given a fair opportunity to present his case; or

    (c) where the judgment is contrary to the public policy of the Contracting Party within the territory of which recognition is sought, or is not in accord with fundamental standards of justice.

2. A final judgment which is recognised shall, upon being presented for enforcement in accordance with the formalities required by the law of the Contracting Party where enforcement is sought, be enforceable as if it were a judgment of a court of that Contracting Party.

3. The merits of a claim on which the judgment has been given shall not be subject to further proceedings.

Article XIII

This Convention and the national law applicable thereunder shall be applied without any discrimination based upon nationality, domicile, or residence.

Article XIV

Except in respect of measures of execution, jurisdictional immunities under rules of national or international law shall not be invoked in actions under this Convention before the courts competent pursuant to Article XI.

Article XV

The Contracting Parties shall take appropriate measures to ensure that compensation for nuclear damage, interest and costs awarded by a court in connection therewith, insurance and reinsurance premiums and funds provided by insurance, reinsurance or other financial security, or funds provided by the Installation State, pursuant to this Convention, shall be freely transferable into the currency of the Contracting Party within whose territory the damage is suffered, and of the Contracting Party within whose territory the claimant is habitually resident and, as regards insurance or reinsurance premiums and payments, into the currencies specified in the insurance or reinsurance contract.

Article XVI

No person shall be entitled to recover compensation under this Convention to the extent that he has recovered compensation in respect of the same nuclear damage under another international convention on civil liability in the field of nuclear energy.

Article XVII

This Convention shall not, as between the parties to them, affect the application of any international agreements or international conventions in civil liability in the field of nuclear energy in force, or open for signature, ratification or accession at the date on which this Convention is opened for signature.

Article XVIII

This Convention shall not be construed as affecting the rights, if any, of a Contracting Party under the general rules of public international law in respect of nuclear damage.

Article XIX

1. Any Contracting Party entering into an agreement pursuant to subparagraph (b) of paragraph 3 of Article XI shall furnish without delay to the Director-General of the International Atomic Energy Agency for information and dissemination to the other Contracting Parties a copy of such agreement.

2. The Contracting Parties shall furnish to the Director-General for information and dissemination to the other Contracting Parties copies of their respective laws and regulations relating to matters covered by this Convention.

Article XX

Notwithstanding the termination of the application of this Convention to any Contracting Party, either by termination pursuant to Article XXV or by denunciation pursuant to Article XXVI, the provisions of this Convention shall continue to apply to any nuclear damage caused by a nuclear incident occurring before such termination.

Article XXI

This Convention shall be open for signature by the States represented at the International Conference on Civil Liability for Nuclear Damage held in Vienna from 29 April to 19 May 1963.

Article XXII

This Convention shall be ratified, and the instruments of ratification shall be deposited with the Director-General of the International Atomic Energy Agency.

Article XXIII

This Convention shall come into force three months after the deposit of the fifth instrument of ratification, and, in respect of each State ratifying it thereafter, three months after the deposit of the instrument of ratification by that State.

Article XXIV

1. All States Members of the United Nations, or of any of the specialised agencies or of the International Atomic Energy Agency not represented at the International Conference on Civil Liability for Nuclear Damage, held in Vienna from 29 April to 19 May 1963, may accede to this Convention.

2. The instrument of accession shall be deposited with the Director General of the International Atomic Energy Agency.

3. This Convention shall come into force in respect of the acceding State three months after the date of deposit of the instrument of accession of that State but not before the date of the entry into force of this Convention pursuant to Article XXIII.

Article XXV

1. This Convention shall remain in force for a period of ten years from the date of its entry into force. Any Contracting Party may, by giving before the end of that period at least twelve months' notice to that effect to the Director-General of the International Atomic Energy Agency, terminate the application of this Convention to itself at the end of that period of ten years.

2. This Convention shall, after that period of ten years, remain in force for a further period of five years for such Contracting Parties as have not terminated its application pursuant to paragraph 1 of this Article, and thereafter for successive periods of five years each for those Contracting Parties which have not terminated its application at the end of one of such periods, by giving, before the end of one of such periods, at least twelve months' notice to that effect to the Director-General of the International Atomic Energy Agency.

Article XXVI

1. A conference shall be convened by the Director-General of the International Atomic Energy Agency at any time after the expiry of a period of five years from the date of the entry into force of this Convention in order to consider the revision thereof, if one-third of the Contracting Parties express a desire to that effect.

2. Any Contracting Party may denounce this Convention by notification to the Director-General of the International Atomic Agency within a period of twelve months following the first revision conference held pursuant to paragraph 1 of this Article.

3. Denunciation shall take effect one year after the date on which notification to that effect has been received by the Director-General of the International Atomic Energy Agency.

Article XXVII

The Director-General of the International Atomic Energy Agency shall notify the States invited to the International Conference on Civil Liability for Nuclear Damage held in Vienna from 29 April to 19 May 1963 and the States which have acceded to this Convention of the following:

  (a) signatures and instruments of ratification and accession received pursuant to Articles XXI, XXII and XXIV;

(b) the date on which the Convention will come into force pursuant to Article XXIII;

(c) notifications of termination and denunciation received pursuant to Articles XXV and XXVI;

(d) requests for the convening of a revision conference pursuant to Article XXVI.

Article XXVIII

This Convention shall be registered by the Director-General of the International Atomic Energy Agency in accordance with Article 102 of the Charter of the United Nations.

Article XXIX

The original of this Convention, of which the English, French, Russian and Spanish texts are equally authentic, shall be deposited with the Director-General of the International Atomic Energy Agency, who shall issue certified copies.

IN WITNESS WHEREOF, the undersigned Plenipotentiaries, duly authorised thereto, have signed this Convention.

JOINT PROTOCOL RELATING TO THE APPLICATION
OF THE *VIENNA CONVENTION* AND THE *PARIS CONVENTION*

THE CONTRACTING PARTIES,

HAVING REGARD to the *Vienna Convention on Civil Liability for Nuclear Damage* of 21 May 1963;

HAVING REGARD to the *Paris Convention on Third Party Liability in the Field of Nuclear Energy* of 29 July 1960 as amended by the *Additional Protocol of 28 January 1964* and by the *Protocol of 16 November 1982*;

CONSIDERING that the *Vienna Convention* and the *Paris Convention* are similar in substance and that no State is at present a Party to both Conventions;

CONVINCED that adherence to either Convention by Parties to the other Convention could lead to difficulties resulting from the simultaneous application of both Conventions to a nuclear incident; and

DESIROUS to establish a link between the *Vienna Convention* and the *Paris Convention* by mutually extending the benefit of the special regime of civil liability for nuclear damage set forth under each Convention and to eliminate conflicts arising from the simultaneous applications of both Conventions to a nuclear incident;

HAVE AGREED as follows:

Article I

In this Protocol:

(a) *"Vienna Convention"* means the *Vienna Convention on Civil Liability for Nuclear Damage* of 21 May 1963 and any amendment thereto which is in force for a Contracting Party to this Protocol;

(b) *"Paris Convention"* means the *Paris Convention on Third Party Liability in the Field of Nuclear Energy* of 29 July 1960 and any amendment thereto which is in force for a Contracting Party to this Protocol.

198

Article II

For the purpose of this Protocol:

(a) the operator of a nuclear installation situated in the territory of a Party to the *Vienna Convention* shall be liable in accordance with that Convention for nuclear damage suffered in the territory of a Party to both the *Paris Convention* and this Protocol;

(b) the operator of a nuclear installation situated in the territory of a Party to the *Paris Convention* shall be liable in accordance with that Convention for nuclear damage suffered in the territory of a Party to both the *Vienna Convention* and this Protocol.

Article III

1.   Either the *Vienna Convention* or the *Paris Convention* shall apply to a nuclear incident to the exclusion of the other.

2.   In the case of a nuclear incident occurring in a nuclear installation, the applicable Convention shall be that to which the State is a Party within whose territory that installation is situated.

3.   In the case of a nuclear incident outside a nuclear installation and involving nuclear material in the course of carriage, the applicable Convention shall be that to which the State is a Party within whose territory the nuclear installation is situated whose operator is liable pursuant to either Articles II.1(b) and (c) of the *Vienna Convention* or Articles 4(a) and (b) of the *Paris Convention*.

Article IV

1.   Articles I to XV of the *Vienna Convention* shall be applied, with respect to the Contracting Parties to this Protocol which are Parties to the *Paris Convention*, in the same manner as between Parties to the *Vienna Convention*.

2.   Articles 1 to 14 of the *Paris Convention* shall be applied, with respect to the Contracting Parties to this Protocol which are Parties to the *Vienna Convention*, in the same manner as between Parties to the *Paris Convention*.

Article V

This Protocol shall be open for signature, from 21 September 1988 until the date of its entry into force, at the Headquarters of the International Atomic Energy Agency by all States which have signed, ratified or acceded to either the *Vienna Convention* or the *Paris Convention*.

Article VI

1. This Protocol is subject to ratification, acceptance, approval or accession. Instruments of ratification, acceptance or approval shall only be accepted from States Party to either the *Vienna Convention* or the *Paris Convention*. Any such State which has not signed this Protocol may accede to it.

2. The instruments of ratification, acceptance, approval or accession shall be deposited with the Director-General of the International Atomic Energy Agency, who is hereby designated as the depositary of this Protocol.

Article VII

1. This Protocol shall come into force three months after the date of deposit of instruments of ratification, acceptance, approval or accession by at least five States Party to the *Vienna Convention* and five States Party to the *Paris Convention*. For each State ratifying, accepting, approving or acceding to this Protocol after the deposit of the above-mentioned instruments this Protocol shall enter into force three months after the date of deposit of the instrument of ratification, acceptance, approval or accession.

2. This Protocol shall remain in force as long as both the *Vienna Convention* and the *Paris Convention* are in force.

Article VIII

1. Any Contracting Party may denounce this Protocol by written notification to the depositary.

2. Denunciation shall take effect one year after the date on which the notification is received by the depositary.

Article IX

1. Any Contracting Party which ceases to be a Party to either the *Vienna Convention* or the *Paris Convention* shall notify the depositary of the termination of the application of that Convention with respect to it and of the date such termination takes effect.

2. This Protocol shall cease to apply to a Contracting Party which has terminated application of either the *Vienna Convention* or the *Paris Convention* on the date such termination takes effect.

Article X

The depositary shall promptly notify Contracting Parties and States invited to the Conference on the relationship between the *Paris Convention* and the *Vienna Convention* as well as the Secretary-General of the Organisation for Economic Cooperation and Development of:

(a) each signature of this Protocol;

(b) each deposit of an instrument of ratification, acceptance, approval or accession concerning this Protocol;

(c) the entry into force of this Protocol;

(d) any denunciation; and

(e) any information received pursuant to Article IX.

Article XI

The original of this Protocol, of which the Arabic, Chinese, English, French, Russian and Spanish texts are equally authentic, shall be deposited with the depositary, who shall send certified copies to Contracting Parties and States invited to the Conference on the relationship between the *Paris Convention* and the *Vienna Convention* as well as the Secretary-General of the Organisation for Economic Cooperation and Development.

IN WITNESS WHEREOF the undersigned being duly authorised by their respective Governments for that purpose have signed the present Joint Protocol.

DONE at Vienna this twenty-first day of September, one thousand nine hundred and eighty-eight.

MAIN SALES OUTLETS OF OECD PUBLICATIONS
PRINCIPAUX POINTS DE VENTE DES PUBLICATIONS DE L'OCDE

ARGENTINA – ARGENTINE
Carlos Hirsch S.R.L.
Galería Güemes, Florida 165, 4° Piso
1333 Buenos Aires   Tel. (1) 331.1787 y 331.2391
Telefax: (1) 331.1787

AUSTRALIA – AUSTRALIE
D.A. Information Services
648 Whitehorse Road, P.O.B 163
Mitcham, Victoria 3132   Tel. (03) 873.4411
Telefax: (03) 873.5679

AUSTRIA – AUTRICHE
Gerold & Co.
Graben 31
Wien I   Tel. (0222) 533.50.14

BELGIUM – BELGIQUE
Jean De Lannoy
Avenue du Roi 202
B-1060 Bruxelles   Tel. (02) 538.51.69/538.08.41
Telefax: (02) 538.08.41

CANADA
Renouf Publishing Company Ltd.
1294 Algoma Road
Ottawa, ON K1B 3W8   Tel. (613) 741.4333
Telefax: (613) 741.5439
Stores:
61 Sparks Street
Ottawa, ON K1P 5R1   Tel. (613) 238.8985
211 Yonge Street
Toronto, ON M5B 1M4   Tel. (416) 363.3171
Telefax: (416)363.59.63

Les Éditions La Liberté Inc.
3020 Chemin Sainte-Foy
Sainte-Foy, PQ G1X 3V6   Tel. (418) 658.3763
Telefax: (418) 658.3763

Federal Publications Inc.
165 University Avenue, Suite 701
Toronto, ON M5H 3B8   Tel. (416) 860.1611
Telefax: (416) 860.1608

Les Publications Fédérales
1185 Université
Montréal, QC H3B 3A7   Tel. (514) 954.1633
Telefax : (514) 954.1635

CHINA – CHINE
China National Publications Import
Export Corporation (CNPIEC)
16 Gongti E. Road, Chaoyang District
P.O. Box 88 or 50
Beijing 100704 PR   Tel. (01) 506.6688
Telefax: (01) 506.3101

DENMARK – DANEMARK
Munksgaard Book and Subscription Service
35, Nørre Søgade, P.O. Box 2148
DK-1016 København K   Tel. (33) 12.85.70
Telefax: (33) 12.93.87

FINLAND – FINLANDE
Akateeminen Kirjakauppa
Keskuskatu 1, P.O. Box 128
00100 Helsinki

Subscription Services/Agence d'abonnements :
P.O. Box 23
00371 Helsinki   Tel. (358 0) 12141
Telefax: (358 0) 121.4450

FRANCE
OECD/OCDE
Mail Orders/Commandes par correspondance:
2, rue André-Pascal
75775 Paris Cedex 16   Tel. (33-1) 45.24.82.00
Telefax: (33-1) 49.10.42.76
Telex: 640048 OCDE
Orders via Minitel, France only/
Commandes par Minitel, France exclusivement :
36 15 OCDE

OECD Bookshop/Librairie de l'OCDE :
33, rue Octave-Feuillet
75016 Paris   Tel. (33-1) 45.24.81.67
(33-1) 45.24.81.81

Documentation Française
29, quai Voltaire
75007 Paris   Tel. 40.15.70.00
Gibert Jeune (Droit-Économie)
6, place Saint-Michel
75006 Paris   Tel. 43.25.91.19
Librairie du Commerce International
10, avenue d'Iéna
75016 Paris   Tel. 40.73.34.60
Librairie Dunod
Université Paris-Dauphine
Place du Maréchal de Lattre de Tassigny
75016 Paris   Tel. (1) 44.05.40.13
Librairie Lavoisier
11, rue Lavoisier
75008 Paris   Tel. 42.65.39.95
Librairie L.G.D.J. - Montchrestien
20, rue Soufflot
75005 Paris   Tel. 46.33.89.85
Librairie des Sciences Politiques
30, rue Saint-Guillaume
75007 Paris   Tel. 45.48.36.02
P.U.F.
49, boulevard Saint-Michel
75005 Paris   Tel. 43.25.83.40
Librairie de l'Université
12a, rue Nazareth
13100 Aix-en-Provence   Tel. (16) 42.26.18.08
Documentation Française
165, rue Garibaldi
69003 Lyon   Tel. (16) 78.63.32.23
Librairie Decitre
29, place Bellecour
69002 Lyon   Tel. (16) 72.40.54.54

GERMANY – ALLEMAGNE
OECD Publications and Information Centre
August-Bebel-Allee 6
D-53175 Bonn   Tel. (0228) 959.120
Telefax: (0228) 959.12.17

GREECE – GRÈCE
Librairie Kauffmann
Mavrokordatou 9
106 78 Athens   Tel. (01) 32.55.321
Telefax: (01) 36.33.967

HONG-KONG
Swindon Book Co. Ltd.
13–15 Lock Road
Kowloon, Hong Kong   Tel. 366.80.31
Telefax: 739.49.75

HUNGARY – HONGRIE
Euro Info Service
Margitsziget, Európa Ház
1138 Budapest   Tel. (1) 111.62.16
Telefax : (1) 111.60.61

ICELAND – ISLANDE
Mál Mog Menning
Laugavegi 18, Pósthólf 392
121 Reykjavik   Tel. 162.35.23

INDIA – INDE
Oxford Book and Stationery Co.
Scindia House
New Delhi 110001   Tel.(11) 331.5896/5308
Telefax: (11) 332.5993
17 Park Street
Calcutta 700016   Tel. 240832

INDONESIA – INDONÉSIE
Pdii-Lipi
P.O. Box 269/JKSMG/88
Jakarta 12790   Tel. 583467
Telex: 62 875

ISRAEL
Praedicta
5 Shatner Street
P.O. Box 34030
Jerusalem 91430   Tel. (2) 52.84.90/1/2
Telefax: (2) 52.84.93
R.O.Y.
P.O. Box 13056
Tel Aviv 61130   Tél. (3) 49.61.08
Telefax (3) 544.60.39

ITALY – ITALIE
Libreria Commissionaria Sansoni
Via Duca di Calabria 1/1
50125 Firenze   Tel. (055) 64.54.15
Telefax: (055) 64.12.57
Via Bartolini 29
20155 Milano   Tel. (02) 36.50.83
Editrice e Libreria Herder
Piazza Montecitorio 120
00186 Roma   Tel. 679.46.28
Telefax: 678.47.51
Libreria Hoepli
Via Hoepli 5
20121 Milano   Tel. (02) 86.54.46
Telefax: (02) 805.28.86
Libreria Scientifica
Dott. Lucio de Biasio 'Aeiou'
Via Coronelli, 6
20146 Milano   Tel. (02) 48.95.45.52
Telefax: (02) 48.95.45.48

JAPAN – JAPON
OECD Publications and Information Centre
Landic Akasaka Building
2-3-4 Akasaka, Minato-ku
Tokyo 107   Tel. (81.3) 3586.2016
Telefax: (81.3) 3584.7929

KOREA – CORÉE
Kyobo Book Centre Co. Ltd.
P.O. Box 1658, Kwang Hwa Moon
Seoul   Tel. 730.78.91
Telefax: 735.00.30

MALAYSIA – MALAISIE
Co-operative Bookshop Ltd.
University of Malaya
P.O. Box 1127, Jalan Pantai Baru
59700 Kuala Lumpur
Malaysia   Tel. 756.5000/756.5425
Telefax: 757.3661

MEXICO – MEXIQUE
Revistas y Periodicos Internacionales S.A. de C.V.
Florencia 57 - 1004
Mexico, D.F. 06600   Tel. 207.81.00
Telefax : 208.39.79

NETHERLANDS – PAYS-BAS
SDU Uitgeverij Plantijnstraat
Externe Fondsen
Postbus 20014
2500 EA's-Gravenhage   Tel. (070) 37.89.880
Voor bestellingen: Telefax: (070) 34.75.778

NEW ZEALAND
NOUVELLE-ZÉLANDE
Legislation Services
P.O. Box 12418
Thorndon, Wellington Tel. (04) 496.5652
Telefax: (04) 496.5698

NORWAY – NORVÈGE
Narvesen Info Center – NIC
Bertrand Narvesens vei 2
P.O. Box 6125 Etterstad
0602 Oslo 6 Tel. (022) 57.33.00
Telefax: (022) 68.19.01

PAKISTAN
Mirza Book Agency
65 Shahrah Quaid-E-Azam
Lahore 54000 Tel. (42) 353.601
Telefax: (42) 231.730

PHILIPPINE – PHILIPPINES
International Book Center
5th Floor, Filipinas Life Bldg.
Ayala Avenue
Metro Manila Tel. 81.96.76
Telex 23312 RHP PH

PORTUGAL
Livraria Portugal
Rua do Carmo 70-74
Apart. 2681
1200 Lisboa Tel.: (01) 347.49.82/5
Telefax: (01) 347.02.64

SINGAPORE – SINGAPOUR
Gower Asia Pacific Pte Ltd.
Golden Wheel Building
41, Kallang Pudding Road, No. 04-03
Singapore 1334 Tel. 741.5166
Telefax: 742.9356

SPAIN – ESPAGNE
Mundi-Prensa Libros S.A.
Castelló 37, Apartado 1223
Madrid 28001 Tel. (91) 431.33.99
Telefax: (91) 575.39.98

Libreria Internacional AEDOS
Consejo de Ciento 391
08009 – Barcelona Tel. (93) 488.30.09
Telefax: (93) 487.76.59
Llibreria de la Generalitat
Palau Moja
Rambla dels Estudis, 118
08002 – Barcelona
(Subscripcions) Tel. (93) 318.80.12
(Publicacions) Tel. (93) 302.67.23
Telefax: (93) 412.18.54

SRI LANKA
Centre for Policy Research
c/o Colombo Agencies Ltd.
No. 300-304, Galle Road
Colombo 3 Tel. (1) 574240, 573551-2
Telefax: (1) 575394, 510711

SWEDEN – SUÈDE
Fritzes Information Center
Box 16356
Regeringsgatan 12
106 47 Stockholm Tel. (08) 690.90.90
Telefax: (08) 20.50.21

Subscription Agency/Agence d'abonnements :
Wennergren-Williams Info AB
P.O. Box 1305
171 25 Solna Tel. (08) 705.97.50
Téléfax : (08) 27.00.71

SWITZERLAND – SUISSE
Maditec S.A. (Books and Periodicals - Livres
et périodiques)
Chemin des Palettes 4
Case postale 266
1020 Renens Tel. (021) 635.08.65
Telefax: (021) 635.07.80

Librairie Payot S.A.
4, place Pépinet
CP 3212
1002 Lausanne Tel. (021) 341.33.48
Telefax: (021) 341.33.45

Librairie Unilivres
6, rue de Candolle
1205 Genève Tel. (022) 320.26.23
Telefax: (022) 329.73.18

Subscription Agency/Agence d'abonnements :
Dynapresse Marketing S.A.
38 avenue Vibert
1227 Carouge Tel.: (022) 308.07.89
Telefax : (022) 308.07.99

See also – Voir aussi :
OECD Publications and Information Centre
August-Bebel-Allee 6
D-53175 Bonn (Germany) Tel. (0228) 959.120
Telefax: (0228) 959.12.17

TAIWAN – FORMOSE
Good Faith Worldwide Int'l. Co. Ltd.
9th Floor, No. 118, Sec. 2
Chung Hsiao E. Road
Taipei Tel. (02) 391.7396/391.7397
Telefax: (02) 394.9176

THAILAND – THAÏLANDE
Suksit Siam Co. Ltd.
113, 115 Fuang Nakhon Rd.
Opp. Wat Rajbopith
Bangkok 10200 Tel. (662) 225.9531/2
Telefax: (662) 222.5188

TURKEY – TURQUIE
Kültür Yayinlari Is-Türk Ltd. Sti
Atatürk Bulvari No. 191/Kat 13
Kavaklidere/Ankara Tel. 428.11.40 Ext. 2458
Dolmabahce Cad. No. 29
Besiktas/Istanbul Tel. 260.71.88
Telex: 43482B

UNITED KINGDOM – ROYAUME-UNI
HMSO
Gen. enquiries Tel. (071) 873 0011
Postal orders only:
P.O. Box 276, London SW8 5DT
Personal Callers HMSO Bookshop
49 High Holborn, London WC1V 6HB
Telefax: (071) 873 8200
Branches at: Belfast, Birmingham, Bristol, Edin-
burgh, Manchester

UNITED STATES – ÉTATS-UNIS
OECD Publications and Information Centre
2001 L Street N.W., Suite 700
Washington, D.C. 20036-4910 Tel. (202) 785.6323
Telefax: (202) 785.0350

VENEZUELA
Libreria del Este
Avda F. Miranda 52, Aptdo. 60337
Edificio Galipán
Caracas 106 Tel. 951.1705/951.2307/951.1297
Telegram: Libreste Caracas

Subscription to OECD periodicals may also be
placed through main subscription agencies.

Les abonnements aux publications périodiques de
l'OCDE peuvent être souscrits auprès des
principales agences d'abonnement.

Orders and inquiries from countries where Distributors have not yet been appointed should be sent to:
OECD Publications Service, 2 rue André-Pascal,
75775 Paris Cedex 16, France.

Les commandes provenant de pays où l'OCDE n'a
pas encore désigné de distributeur peuvent être
adressées à : OCDE, Service des Publications,
2, rue André-Pascal, 75775 Paris Cedex 16, France.

11-1994

OECD PUBLICATIONS, 2 rue André-Pascal, 75775 PARIS CEDEX 16
PRINTED IN FRANCE
(66 94 12 1) ISBN 92-64-14280-0 - No. 47531 1994